This book is for you...

- If you enjoy writing

- If you want to enter more competitions

- If you suffer from writer's block

- If you would like to write more stories, but lack the ideas

- If the sight of a blank page makes your blood run cold

- If your twist endings don't quite work

- If you have never written fiction, but would like to

- If you yearn for easy-to-read no-nonsense advice

"Forsooth, I could have written six more plays had this book been available in the 16th Century."
William Shakespeare, 1599

"With this book to aid me, my pilgrims could have made another trip to Canterbury, and back!"
Geoffrey Chaucer, 1382

"This is a Dickens of a good book!"
Charles, 1855

The Writer's Treasury of Ideas

By Linda Lewis

Filament Publishing

Published by Filament Publishing Ltd
16, Croydon Road, Waddon,
Croydon, Surrey, CR0 4PA UK
Telephone +44 (0)20 8688 2598
Fax +44 (0)20 7183 7186
info@filamentpublishing.com
www.filamentpublishing.com

© Linda Lewis 2012

Printed by Berforts Group - Stevenage and Hastings
Distributed by Gardners

ISBN 978-1-908691-11-8

Dedicated to the memory of Gareth Lewis and Christina Waugh, two of the best.

MAGNUM OCTOPUS

CONTENT

About the Author – Linda Lewis

Linda was born in London, moving to Leeds (via Devon) in 2009.

Her writing career began in 1990 when she signed up for a correspondence course. One assignment was to write an article about something she knew about. She chose tropical fish. That first piece went on to be published and for the next seven years she wrote more and more articles about tropical fish for magazines in the UK, USA and South Africa. At the same time, she began to write fillers – the short pieces of writing that magazines use to fill up their pages.

When her husband died, in 1997, she began to switch her focus to fiction, selling her first story to *Take a Break* in 1998. That was when she started to use the pen name, Catherine Howard.

Since 2003, she has been working full time as a writer, concentrating mainly on short stories. Her stories have been published in the following magazines – *Fiction Feast, Best, Chat, That's Life, Woman, Yours, Take A Break, Woman's Weekly, My Weekly, The Weekly News, Ireland's Own* as well as magazines in Sweden, Norway, Denmark and Australia. Her first story for *The People's Friend* is due to be published sometime in 2012. She has lost count of how many stories she has sold, guessing that the number is somewhere between two and three hundred.

In 2008, she was given a column in Writers' Forum, entitled *Short Story Success*, in which she passes on tips to other fiction writers, and tells them about her life as a working writer.

In 2011, her first novel, *The Magic Of Fishkeeping*, was published. That was also the year that her life changed direction. Due to major problems in her personal life, she began to move away from fiction and switched her focus to non-fiction, producing three short writers' guides, and working on an autobiography. She also began to develop other interests, including teaching. In 2011, she ran a workshop on writing fillers at Swanwick Writers' Summer School and is due to teach the short story course there in 2012. She will also be teaching at the NAWG Festival of Writing and at a weekend residential course in Leeds in November 2012 (www.malagaworkshops.co.uk).

She also offers a critique service and tailor-made writing lessons, helps organise and judge short story competitions, and gives talks to all kinds of groups on a variety of subjects including what it's really like to appear on television quiz shows! Linda was lucky enough to win *The Weakest Link*, and has also appeared on ITV1's *The Chase*.

To find out more about Linda's work, including her feedback service, talks, and writing courses, visit her website www.akacatherinehoward.weebly.com. She can also be followed on Twitter at writingiseasy

Introduction

How do you find ideas for your stories and books? Admit it. The last time you met a successful writer, you asked them that, didn't you?

Everybody knows the mechanics of writing; it's one of the very first things we learn to do at school, second only to reading. Pushing a pen over the page or pressing buttons on a keyboard is a simple task that most of us can manage with ease.

It's coming up with ideas that can cause difficulties. This book will help you solve that problem.

We all like to think that if we'd thought of *Discworld* before Terry Pratchett did, we'd be sitting on top of the bestsellers list year in, year out. And whoever thought that J.K. Rowling's simple story about a boy wizard would have such an amazing impact?

Writing has never been more popular. It seems that everybody is giving it a go. The internet is positively groaning under the weight of blogs.

More than ever before, there are opportunities for writers everywhere - writing jokes for comedy shows, slogans for advertising campaigns or poems for greeting cards, to name just a few. There are also literally thousands of short story and poetry competitions every year offering a total prize fund of millions of pounds.

New magazines come out every month, and despite all the protestations of doom, people are buying as many books as ever they did. Electronic books haven't killed off the printed kind and probably never will. Technology is moving so fast, it's hard to say what will happen, but what seems certain is that people will always want to read. What form that reading takes is by the by.

As a full time writer, I need a constant supply of fresh ideas otherwise my stories and articles will not catch an editor's eye and I would soon be in trouble.

When I'm in short story writing mode, I need to write at least two stories every week. That means I have to have a constant supply of fresh ideas. To be able to do that, I have trained myself to the point where I can find ideas almost everywhere.

This book will give you an insight into the ways and means, some simple, some straightforward, and others downright devious, that I use to generate ideas. Best of all, it will show you how to use them.

Some people say that there are only a dozen or so plots in the whole world, and that all writers do is take these old plots and give them a tweak.

Other people think that if you sit down and think long and hard enough, an idea will come to you, but it rarely happens like that. Sometimes the harder you try to think of something, the more impossible it is.

The truth is that ideas rain down on us, mostly when we aren't expecting them. The problem that most people face is that they have very big umbrellas. Ideas simply bounce off them, without being noticed.

Ideas are tricky things. They're ephemeral. You can't see them, or take hold of them. They're also invisible, but like radio waves, they're everywhere. Read this book and you will soon realise that.

There is a huge amount of information contained in this book. My advice is to read it through first of all, then go through it again, trying each method in turn. That's the best way to find the tricks and techniques that work for you.

Then, with any luck, the next big idea will be one of yours.

Questions

Questions are the key that writers use to unlock new ideas. Ask enough of them and you will have all the ideas you ever need, and if you're like me, more than you could hope to use in a lifetime. You may find it hard at first, but like any skill, the more you practise, the easier it becomes.

The 'Five Ws' (and one H) were immortalised by Rudyard Kipling in his *Just So Stories* (1902), in which a poem accompanying the tale of *The Elephant's Child* opens with:

> *I keep six honest serving-men*
> *(They taught me all I knew);*
> *Their names are What and Why and When*
> *And How and Where and Who.*

Luckily human beings are, by their very nature, curious about things. All you have to do is develop this natural trait.

Of the six questions mentioned in Kipling's poem, my favourite has to be "Why?"

Children like that question too, as anyone with a family can testify. Children ask "Why?" over and over again, especially when trying to avoid doing something they don't want to do – "Why do I have to go to bed now?", "Why are carrots good for me?" and so on.

Therapists also ask "Why?" quite a lot in order to help their clients or patients to understand themselves and therefore move towards feeling better or resolving a problem. If you're stuck for a story idea, just keep asking "Why?" questions until you start to move forward.

"Why?" gets straight to the heart of the matter. "Why do I have to go to school?" "Why do you want to lose weight?"

On the surface, these might look like simple questions, but they're actually filled with meaning. If you want to come up with enough ideas to keep you in story plots for years to come, keep asking "Why?"

Why is that person sad/happy/angry? Why do they put up with their sister/partner/parents? Why do they keep making the same mistakes? Why did he murder his wife? Why did they hate each other? And so on.

Until you know what motivates your characters, any stories they appear in will not work as well as they could.

I am often disappointed with TV detective stories because the motive they give for somebody committing murder doesn't ring true. For me, motive is far more important (and interesting) than means and opportunity. Like a child, I want to know why.

Means and opportunity lead naturally to the next question – "How?"

This question is vital if we want to make sure that our story works in a logical way. How did the heroine suddenly get to the kitchen when last time they spoke, they were in the garden? How does the man know about the affair, or which poisons work fastest?

As regards to fiction, questions beginning with "What" can be incredibly useful. My particular favourite is, "What is the character's secret?" and "What is it they don't want their friends or family to know?"

Another one I use all the time is, "What do they really want and what is preventing them from achieving it?"

As you read this book, the question of conflict will keep cropping up.

Stories are all about problems and how people try, or fail, or learn to compromise, on their way to solving them.

Often the real reason is buried. A woman might tell her friends and family that she wants a part time job to earn some extra money to buy clothes, but delve deeper and you may discover that she needs to get out of the house because her out of work partner is getting on her nerves or is abusive.

Another possibility is that she doesn't need the money. She may have taken a job because she is lonely and wants to make friends.

I have a lodger. If you were to ask me why, I might say that the money he pays for his room helps me financially, but the real reason I rent out my spare room is because living on my own doesn't suit me.

There are all kinds of reasons for this. One I'm happy to share is that having somebody to cater for means that I eat better meals than I would if I was only cooking for me. Other reasons may be so deeply buried that even I don't know the answer.

Try asking yourself these questions. What is it you really want? Do you already have it? If not, what is getting in the way?

Do you have a secret that nobody knows, not even your nearest and dearest?

As you think about the answers to these questions, certain basic truths about you will emerge. These basic truths are what help us to understand ourselves, and why we do the things we do. It stands to reason that if we know the basic truths about our characters, they will become far more real, both to us and to our readers.

As you read on, keep asking questions, questions, and more questions, and you will start coming up with ideas. It really is that simple.

Your Own Life (And Work)

An obvious place to look for ideas is our own life experience.

When we stop to think about it, our lives are full of stories, but because we are so close to them, we might not always see that they are there.

Over the years, you will have faced very many problems and difficulties in your life which, if you were lucky, you overcame.

Each one of these holds the germ of a potential story. Remember that problems don't have to be big or difficult to be interesting to other people.

Exercise

Make a note of five problems you have faced, and overcome, in your life. Would any of these make a story?

Some people find this hard, so let me give you some hints.

Did you ever fall in love with somebody who your parents did not approve of? What happened? Did you go on to marry them?

Did you suffer from any illnesses, either as a child or as an adult, or lose a family member or a spouse?

Did you ever have difficulty learning a new skill or passing a test?

Was there ever somebody at work that you really did not get on with, however hard you tried?

Next, you might want to think about some of the relationships you've had with other people.

For example, a man might think of himself as a husband and father first, but he may have many other roles as well – brother, uncle, neighbour, boss, employee, member of the darts team. Any of these roles can make a great main character for a story.

Many writers always use their own lives as the inspiration for their fiction, others hardly ever do it. It comes down to personal taste and your own reasons for writing short stories.

Until recently, I wrote fiction as a way of escaping from reality. It's only lately that I've started to make use of some of the ups and downs of my own life.

It's up to you how you feel, but I have a word of warning here. If you write about things that really happened, you need to ensure that they make good fiction.

I have read many stories that were based on the truth that simply didn't work. Why is this? One reason is that in real life, coincidences happen all the time. Events don't follow in a logical progression.

In short, life doesn't have a structure. If you stick too closely to the truth, you may find the story lacks form. Simply put, that often means that the ending of the story bears no relation to the beginning.

The most satisfying stories have a shape to them. Often the action goes round in a kind of circle, coming back to a point very close to where they started but with one crucial difference – something about the main character or their circumstances has changed.

It's important to remember that storytelling is not about telling the truth. The word fiction actually means lies.

According to one of my dictionaries, fiction is the act of feigning or imagining that which does not exist or is not actual. That explains why many radio and television programmes that concern real people or events are 'dramatised'. In other words, liberties are taken with the facts to make them more entertaining and interesting.

So bear this in mind when using your own life as a basis for stories. You might need to change the beginning, the middle, the ending, or all three to make a satisfying story.

Basing characters on real people can actually be very limiting because real people behave in certain ways, peculiar to them.

If I based a fictional character on John Lennon, I would find myself asking, "What would John do in this situation?" when I was writing a story.

What we need is for the character to do what's natural for them and that's often much easier if they are completely made up.

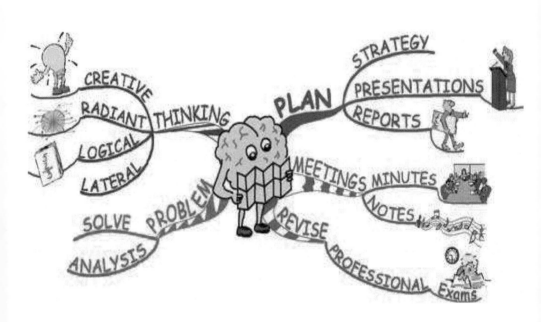

Mind Mapping

Mind mapping is an easy to use, very effective technique that can be of enormous help to writers.

A mind map is a visual diagram which allows you to develop ideas. This technique is simple, but hard to explain in words. One way to think about it is to visualise a tree. The theme or basic idea forms the trunk. From the trunk grow branches, which split into smaller branches, finally ending up as twigs.

For example, if I needed an idea for a Christmas story, I would take a large sheet of paper and sketch the trunk of a tree. I would label this 'Christmas'. Now I would add branches. These might be labelled 'family', 'presents', 'Father Christmas' or anything else that comes to mind. From these branches, other offshoots would grow. Presents might lead to 'last minute shopping', family might lead to 'squabbles' and so on.

Eventually I will have a tree with many branches and offshoots, giving me plenty of themes and subjects I can work on, all leading back to the central theme I started with.

For a much clearer explanation, go to wikipedia (www.wikipedia.org) or take a look at *Turning Your Knowledge into Income* by Chris Day, which features an excellent chapter written by Phil Chambers, a mind mapping champion.

The book is available from Filament Publishing, ISBN 978-1-905493-40-1. A quick internet search will also reveal a wide range of computer software, much of which is free to use.

Mind mapping is not only useful for fiction, it's brilliant for non fiction too. I used the technique when I wrote about tropical fish. When I started writing about them, I was sure I would run out of ideas within a couple of years, but with mind mapping to help me, that didn't happen.

When you try it, the important thing is to be relaxed and let yourself go with the flow. Whatever comes into your mind, write it down on the map without stopping to think. Even if the idea seems crazy, put it on the map. You may soon find out that it is not as crazy as you first thought as more and more links and connections start to form.

I could end here because I've already covered the most important ways that you can use to come up with ideas.

The remainder of the book is arranged as an A-Z, covering many of the different methods that can be used to inspire ideas.

As you read on, you will soon see just how many different ways there are to kick start your imagination. All you need to do is remember to keep asking those questions, and using mind maps, then, like me, you need never run out of ideas again.

Adverts

We are flooded by adverts day in, day out. Most people don't take much notice of them, but I do. I see them as possible starting points for stories, articles or readers' letters.

Next time you're watching a commercial TV station, instead of skipping through the ads or going out of the room and putting the kettle on, try watching them carefully.

A writer, in need of an idea, will not see an advert as an annoying interruption. Instead they might try looking at it as though it was a short play.

For an advert to make an impact it needs that extra special something. It may be humour, or conflict between the characters. These are exactly the things that a successful short story needs. The most useful ones are those where two or more people interact.

For example, there was an advert for a certain make of car a while back in which two young boys talk and act like adults, whilst the grown-ups either drop things or play games. This would make an ideal set-up for a twist in the tale story where the reader is led to assume that the main characters are adults, when they are in fact children.

Short story writers can learn an awful lot from studying adverts. Ads need to be simple and easy to understand if they are to get their message across successfully.

Time is money on television so they have to be concise and compact. They can't afford to spend a minute setting up the situation. They have to grab the viewer's attention straightway to ensure they keep watching. Their aim is to deliver a simple and easy to understand message that is both effective and lingers in the mind.

This is exactly what I aim to do when I write a short story so the next time the adverts come on, ask yourself this question – is what you are watching a basis for a story? Is there a beginning, a middle and an end? Are there any twists? Have the normal (male and female, old and young) roles been reversed? If so, you are looking at a great starting point for an idea.

Adverts are useful in other ways too. They tell you a great deal about the public, especially what they are worried about at the moment. Trends change. Right now there are dozens of adverts for beauty products – miracle anti-ageing creams, hair dye, skin care – for men as well as women.

Other popular themes are healthy foods – probiotics and so on, and cleaning products that can wipe out every germ known to man. If these are the things people care, or worry and fret about, then any writer who uses these themes in a short story has a much greater chance of making a connection with a reader, and as a result, a better chance of impressing an editor or a competition judge, and getting that story published.

Adverts also reveal things about the society we live in today. Go back to the sixties and women would more often than not be seen in the kitchen or caring for children. Now the roles are less well defined.

Think of that advert where two large hairy men dressed as women compete to see which of them is using the better kitchen towel. It works because it's fun, and it's memorable, but if it had been aired thirty years ago, people would probably not have seen the joke.

Advertisers don't like to pass up a chance to influence us and sell us their products. Nowadays you can find screens showing adverts in many post offices, they've even crept into some supermarkets. If you go out for a walk, you are bombarded with billboards, posters at bus stops, even on the tube or in a bus; the adverts are there, shouting at us. Mostly we don't give them much thought. We walk on by, turn the page, or resolutely try and avert our eyes.

Newspapers and magazines are crammed full of adverts – it's how the publishers make their money.

Think about adverts in magazines for a moment. Like those on television, they reflect current thinking. More than that, they tell a writer an awful lot about the people who read those magazines.

Imagine you have picked up a magazine and the adverts include the following – stairlifts, comfy slippers and various pieces of equipment designed to make taking a bath easier. Is that magazine targeting teenagers, or older people?

Now take another magazine where the adverts are for expensive clothes and shoes, and exotic holidays. Is this kind of magazine aimed at the well off or people struggling to manage?

You may be thinking, "Hold on a minute, aren't you talking about stereotyping here?" Yes. I'm afraid I am because that's what magazines and newspapers do all the time. They have no choice but to pigeonhole their readers.

Advertisers are paying a lot of money to make sure their ads are seen by the right people – people who want whatever it is the advert is selling (see *Magazines* and *Newspapers*).

They don't want their ad for trainers to appear in a magazine that's only read by people over sixty. Their main market is younger people. It doesn't matter that some older people do wear trainers, they want their advert to be seen by the biggest number of potential buyers possible.

That means, simply by looking at the adverts, writers can see who the publication's target audience is. If their audience is mainly people of pensionable age, a sixty-five year old heroine might go down better with the editor than a thirty year old. That knowledge can make the difference between a sale and a rejection.

So back to the adverts themselves. How can adverts in newspapers and magazines give writers ideas? The short answer is not all of them do – it's hard to get inspired about ads that simply state the facts. The most useful are those that include people.

Here in the UK, everybody knows the DFS ads where gorgeous sofas are offered at discount prices.

Next time you see one of their ads in the paper, look at the people in them, then ask yourself some basic questions. Why are they buying a sofa? Have they just moved, or won some money? If they are a couple, does one want to buy and the other not? What about their old sofa? Does it hold lots of happy memories?

See how simple it is to start to build up a story? You can do this with almost any product, just by asking that most simple of questions – "WHY?" Why are they buying this? Is it a good idea? Is their partner or parent or offspring happy about it?

Even something as mundane as an advert for shoe polish can get the little grey cells working if you ask yourself – "Why?"

Adverts can be used to generate ideas for articles too. Going back to DFS, has anybody written an article about sofas lately? Think for a minute. What's involved in sofa manufacture? Have fashions changed much in recent years? What's the history behind seating? Why is the chaise longue no longer as popular? What is the most money that's been paid for a sofa?

With a bit of research, any of these might yield an article. The market for this might be any one of dozens of magazines dealing with anything from furniture to home decorating to history.

Now to give you an example of how the process actually works.

One day, I happened to think about the thousands of sofas that DFS must sell. Then I started to wonder what happened to all the old ones that were being replaced.

The following short story was the result. It has been published in the UK and in Australia.

A SOFA OF MEMORIES

"That all seems fine, Mrs Andrews." The auctioneer gave her his card. *"The van will be here tomorrow at ten. There's just one small problem - the sofa."*

"The sofa? What's wrong with it?"

"It's too old. I don't think it will sell, and we can't risk getting stuck with it."

"Oh dear. I need everything to go. The new owners move in on Friday, and I have to get back to Lincoln."

The man thought for a moment. "If it doesn't sell, we could take it to the tip, but there'd have to be a charge. Say £25?"

"OK," she said brightly. "Bye," but as she closed the door, her eyes filled with tears.

"Don't be daft," she told herself. "It's just an old sofa. Why are you getting so upset?"

But she couldn't help it. It was as if all the pain involved in clearing out her mother's house had suddenly come to the surface.

Her thoughts drifted back to the day the sofa was delivered, along with its strange, new, leather smell. She must have been five years old.

Her father was prouder than a peacock; the sofa was the first major piece of furniture he had ever bought new.

The whole family had gathered round, admiring the chocolate brown leather, too overwhelmed even to touch it.

At last Marjorie's mother plonked herself down, and patted the space beside her. Then they'd all piled on together - her parents, her brother and her two sisters, and dissolved into helpless giggles.

With each passing year, the sofa had grown softer and more comfortable. So it was a bit battered, and the leather was getting thin, but it wasn't torn, and there were only a few, small stains here and there. Nothing that couldn't be covered by a carefully placed cushion.

Memories popped into her head like trains arriving at a station.

Saturday evenings, hiding behind the sofa when the Daleks were on Doctor Who.

Afternoons playing pretend, when it would be a horse one minute and a ship the next. The regular rummage down the back and sides of the cushions, hoping to unearth hidden treasures.

The very first time Edward had kissed her, gradually moving closer, inch by inch, while she pretended not to notice. As she thought of her husband, she wondered what he would do if she took the sofa home, but the idea was ridiculous.

It didn't match anything, and they already had more than enough furniture. Besides, how would she get it there? It was much too large for any roof rack.

Just then, the doorbell rang.

Marjorie pulled a Kleenex from her bag, blew her nose, and went to answer it.

It was Susan James, from number 46. They'd been friends at school, and still sent each other cards at Christmas and on birthdays.

"The lights were on," she said, giving her old friend a welcoming hug. "I thought you might need some company."

Her kind words started Marjorie's tears again.

"Sit yourself down," ordered Susan. "I'll make a brew."

As the tea worked its magic, Marjorie began to feel better. "Thanks for coming over," she said.

"I remember how I felt when my mother died," said Susan. "All those memories - it can be very painful and I didn't have a house to clear."

Marjorie wiped her eyes. "I was fine until the auctioneer said he couldn't take the sofa. I can't bear to think of it being thrown away. My brother and sisters have already taken what they wanted." She sniffed. "Dad would be so upset."

"Well he's not here and you are. Besides, somebody's bound to spot it, and take it home. Chesterfields never really go out of fashion." She paused to finish her drink. "When me and Bert got married, we furnished our first flat with things other folk had thrown out."

"Really?"

She nodded. "And nothing can take your memories away, you'll always have those."

Susan got up and headed off to the kitchen. "I spotted an opened bottle of wine in the fridge. Why don't we finish it off?"

When Marjorie woke the next morning, she recalled Susan's words. Her friend was right. It was just a sofa. Memories were much more important.

Later, when the auctioneers were nearly finished, she packed her car and got ready to leave. There was only the old sofa left to move.

The men had just carried it out on to the pavement, when a young man came running down the road, his girlfriend not far behind.

He spoke in short gasps, as he recovered from his run. "I'm Daniel. Aunt Susan called me." He pointed to the young woman who had just caught up. "Me and Katie have just got our first place. We've hardly got any furniture. Can we buy your sofa?"

"If you want it, you're welcome to it," said Marjorie.

"Wow," said the girl as she sat down. She ran her hand over the plump cushions. "It's so soft."

"It's perfect," said Daniel. "Real leather, isn't it?"

Marjorie nodded.

"I've only got £30. Is that enough?" he asked as he pulled the notes from his pocket.

She smiled. "I don't want anything for it. I just want it to have a good home."

"Thanks ever so much," said the young man. "It's exactly what we need."

"How do you plan to move it?" asked Marjorie.

At that moment, four young men arrived in a white Peugeot Estate.

Daniel grinned. "I called for reinforcements, just in case," he said.

"But you'll never get it in there," exclaimed Marjorie.

"No need. Our place isn't far," replied the girl. "We can carry it."

Then at the young man's command, he and his friends lifted up the sofa and began to make their way, slowly but steadily, down the street.

Every few yards, they stopped and took turns to sit on the sofa for a rest. Katie chose to walk a couple of paces behind. Sensible lass, thought Marjorie with a smile.

When they were on the move, all she could see were the young men's feet sticking out at the bottom of the sofa. It looked as though a giant fat brown caterpillar was wobbling its way down the road.

She was laughing as she shut the front door for the last time.

The old sofa had given her another happy memory to take back home.

Agony and Advice Columns

One thing short story writers learn, quite early in their career, is that short stories need conflict. In short, the main character (or characters) needs to have a problem of some kind. The problems can be major – large debts, addiction, infidelity, and so on, or relatively minor – they can't decide where to go on holiday, or what to wear.

Once you have given your character a problem, the story comes from their attempts to solve it. So where do you find a problem? One of the obvious solutions is the advice column in a magazine or newspaper. The great thing is that not only do you get a ready made problem, you also get some tips towards the solution.

Problems vary in both seriousness and tone, according to which magazine or newspaper you select. My favourite is Mrs Mills from the back page of *The Sunday Times Magazine*. The advice she offers is frequently rude and often risqué. It's plain that the problems have all been made up to fit the column, but, and this is an important but, they are still problems.

Advice columns vary enormously, each one being tailored to fit the style of the publication. Sometimes celebrities write the replies with varying degrees of usefulness. (Graham Norton and Ozzy Osbourne have both been agony aunts)

You may wonder how much help some of the replies actually are, or whether the problems they advise on are real or fictitious, but none of this matters to you.

As a writer, they are simply a gold mine. Even an outrageous solution courtesy of Mrs Mills can help you to think of a problem in a different way. Fiction may be about solving problems, but if your character solves them too easily or in the most obvious way, your story may suffer.

Next time you pick up a magazine or newspaper, read the problem pages. As you do, imagine the person who has written in and start asking those all important questions.

Is there more to the problem than meets the eye? What has caused the problem? What do you think they will do to try and solve it? Will they follow the advice they're given? Do they actually WANT to solve the problem?

If this doesn't spark off an idea, have a think about the person giving the advice.

What kind of person are they? What is their motivation? Is it money or prestige, or are they the kind of person who gives advice when it's not needed, who always thinks they know best? What makes them qualified to give advice? Are they, in fact, qualified? What's going on in THEIR lives? Is everything as perfect as they make out?

I wrote a story about a woman who had a monthly column in a newspaper where she told the world about her perfect life as a homemaker. Unfortunately, it was all a complete fabrication. This becomes clear when her editor asks her to let a fashion photographer stay with her and her family as he's a big fan of the column.

The woman has told the world about her wonderful life in a big house with two dogs, and a wonderful husband, when she actually lives alone, in a small terrace.

The story tells how she goes about solving the problem.

I won't tell you how it ends as you might want to take this idea and use it yourself. It doesn't need to be an advice column; it could be somebody who sets themselves up as a great cook when it's really their spouse who's the chef, or a man who writes about his family life when he's recently separated from his wife. This same basic idea can be used over and over.

I hope you get the idea.

Here's an **Exercise** to get you started.

Find an agony column and choose a problem that you know something about. Imagine that you are the person with that problem. Don't worry about the age or gender. Now write a story showing them dealing with the problem following the advice they've been given in the column.

Now ask yourself this question – can I give the ending some kind of twist? Maybe the person decided to do the exact opposite or they realise that the problem no longer worries them. That may be enough to give that extra layer of interest that can turn the story into a winner.

Animals

Do you have any pets?

Most people like animals, so using them in our stories can give writers an advantage.

A sense of place can make a great starting point for a story idea, so if you do have pets, where did you get them from? A puppy farm, a pet shop, a rescue centre? Any one of these would make a good setting.

Now for the people. Did you meet anybody while you were there? Do they have a story to tell? A few examples might be a woman who works at the rescue centre, but has no dogs of her own because she gets too attached to them. Or the dog breeder who takes his job too seriously to the extent that his marriage suffers. Or the shop assistant who wants that particular guinea pig/tortoise/rabbit for themselves and tries to talk any potential customers out of buying.

Dogs and cats often feature in stories, but there are other animals too. Think about all the different kinds of birds that people keep as pets and don't forget the millions of people who keep fish or have ponds in their gardens.

Horses are also popular. Where did you last see one? In a field, at a riding school, on the road – all of these can cause their own particular problems to the people who encounter them.

Take care when choosing less popular animals like snakes or mice, as you risk alienating readers who find them frightening. That said, handled carefully, most animals can be made to seem appealing. Take toads for example. *Toad of Toad Hall* has been a popular fictional hero for decades.

Animals often feature in news stories in local papers and on television as they have that wonderful "aah" factor.

Next time you see one, cut it out or make a note in your ideas book. See if you can develop the piece into a story about a dog that saved the day, or warned its owner of danger, or sniffed out an illness.

I once saw a programme about a dog that made a habit of sitting with people the night before they died. That started me thinking. What if they started to think that the dog was causing the deaths in some way?

I ended up writing a story where a dog keeps being brought back to the rescue centre because his owners end up dead. The story was almost five thousand words long and appeared in *Take a Break's Fiction Feast*. If you'd like to read it, it's called *Saving Sam* and it's in my short story collection, *Crime Shorts Too*.

Now think about the different genres of stories and see whether a story about a dog (or any other animal) might give you an unusual angle. For example, instead of a human, why not have a dog as a ghost? Or give a dog to a character you might not expect to have one, like a cowboy or a clown.

A few years ago, stories told from the viewpoint of a character who, at the end, is revealed to be an animal, were popular with editors.

One of my favourites is Daphne du Maurier's *The Old Man*. I'm not going to spoil it for you. If you want to read it, you can find it at the library in a collection called *The Birds and Other Stories*, or on the internet.

Sadly, fashions change and this kind of story is currently out of favour, but you might be able to use the idea for a children's story.

Exercise

Make a few notes about all the animals you have kept as pets, not just cats and dogs.

Is there a story, ready and waiting? As memories don't always work as well as we'd like them to, this exercise is best tackled over a few days, longer even, as those forgotten pets find their way back to you. If no stories emerge, the time hasn't been wasted as you're almost certain to have found at least a filler.

Fillers are those very short pieces of writing – letters, tips, anecdotes and so on, that magazines use to fill any odd spaces. Sometimes whole pages are devoted to them. Anything about cute or cuddly animals is always popular.

Blurbs

Blurbs are the bits on the back of books that tell us just enough about them to make us want to part with our money.

Blurbs tell us the basic information we need to decide whether this might be the kind of book we would want to read. This information might include when and where the story is set, the age range of the people concerned and what kind of book it is, for example if it falls into a particular genre such as romance or crime.

With novels, they usually tell you a bit about the main character and what their circumstances are and what kind of problems they are facing. There will also be a few hints about what is going to happen to them.

Sometimes, stories in magazines also have very short blurbs. These can be a line taken from the story, or a few words designed to make people want to read it. This example comes from *The People's Friend*.

'Susan's relationship with her husband was wonderful. If it wasn't for the other woman in his life, it might have been perfect.'

This being *The People's Friend*, we can be fairly sure that the other woman is not the man's mistress. She's more likely to be his mother, which turns out to be the case, but she could be his boss, his daughter, or his sister. Until you read on, you can't know for certain.

The following are examples from some of my stories that were published in *Woman's Weekly*.

'It was my idea to get out the old home videos. And for the first half hour or so, Barry and I enjoy them. But then the action switches to my friend Janet's wedding reception – and there's me, with a man who's not my husband.'

'This was the fourth time she'd tried to do this and now her nerve had vanished. Maybe it wasn't such a good idea after all.'

'My daughter had suffered enough since her bereavement. She needed to rejoin the outside world and Steve would make a perfect boyfriend. All I had to do was convince her.'

I hope you will agree that all of these raise questions in a reader's mind. If this happens as you read a blurb, try to resist the temptation to read the story. Instead, start to answer those questions in your own way, then you can write your version of the story.

The way to start might be to ask questions about the kind of person involved. Let's work through these and see how that might work.

In the first example, it's clear that the main character is a woman. She is watching old videos with Barry, who is probably her husband.

What happens next is up to you. You might assume that some kind of confrontation is about to take place, or that the woman will quickly stop the film and try to change the subject. It's up to you to decide if she had an affair or was merely tempted, and it's for you to decide what the husband's role in all of this is.

In my story, the husband had had an affair which his wife was finding impossible to forgive. Seeing the film and how close she came to doing exactly the same thing helps her to forgive and forget. What path does your story take?

In the second example, we know the main character is female and that she has a problem. She's tried to do something before and failed.

The question you need to ask is what is it she has a problem with? Is it something straightforward like a driving test, going on the radio, or giving a talk? What happens next?

In my version, her problem is that she is shy and can't stand up for herself at work. Her inability to say no means that she continually gets taken advantage of. Her solution is to take an assertiveness class where she finally learns how to stand up for herself.

In the third example, the main character is a parent, worried about their daughter. She's probably her mother, but it could just as easily be a father. Whoever the main character is, they seem to have decided that Steve would make a good match for their daughter. Are they right or wrong? How do they try and arrange the match? Does it work out as planned or does somebody else come along?

The tone sounds quite light, but it need not stay that way. Maybe the mother is not the considerate caring person we first thought. Maybe she wants her daughter to get together with Steve for the wrong reasons (he's rich or well connected). Keep asking those questions and the story will emerge. Whether it's anything like my original doesn't matter.

Once you've drafted your version, you can go back to the original story and read it. You will probably find that yours is completely different. Even if there are similarities, it should be different enough to stand on its own.

Books and Book Titles

For a change, I'm starting with an **Exercise**. It goes like this. Choose a fiction book at random, either from your own collection, or a shop or library.

Write down the title then spend five minutes writing a few notes on what the story could be about.

I tried this just now and the first book I spotted was *Northern Lights* by Philip Pullman.

I thought about the amazing displays of light the book is named after, then it was time to bring in a character. Maybe a man had always wanted to see the northern lights and decides to make one last trip before he dies.

Or somebody may have had a job as a guide. He or she had seen the amazing sight so many times, it no longer thrilled them. Do they regain their sense of wonder or has it been lost forever? That's for you, the writer, to decide.

Of course, *Northern Lights* could be something else entirely. It could be the name of a boat or a cottage somewhere nice and spooky. Why not try a mind map and see where it takes you?

Now let's try this with a different book.

How about *The Wind in the Willows*? Is this literally a wind blowing through trees, or is it a supernatural force, or something only the hero can hear? Do they only hear the sound when a certain person is with them? If so, what does it mean?

There has been a tendency recently for people to write follow ups to famous books, or prequels. *The Wide Sargasso Sea*, a prequel to *Jane Eyre*, springs to mind.

If you have a favourite book that is out of copyright, you might want to consider writing a prequel or taking a minor character and telling their story instead.

For example, you might choose Nancy or The Artful Dodger from *Oliver Twist*. If you prefer writing about villains, Bill Sykes and Fagin would make great characters for a book. I for one would want to read either of those.

The beauty of this idea is that you already have most of the plot. Also, working with a character that readers already feel they know is not only intriguing, it saves a lot of groundwork.

Characters

To me, characters are the life blood of a story or film. It doesn't matter how brilliant the plot is, if the characters are made of cardboard, I quickly lose interest.

What I enjoy is seeing how that particular person copes with whatever the plot throws at them. Faced with exactly the same circumstances, everyone responds in different ways; that's what makes people interesting and unique.

Try the following **Exercise**. It takes time and effort, but is well worth doing.

It goes like this. Write a full character outline for a cast of characters. You are not looking for a simple physical description (hair, eye colour, height, weight) but more of a personality profile. What do they do for fun? What hobbies do they have? Do they have any skills or talents? What TV programmes do they like/hate? Do they enjoy sports? Do they have any pet hates or annoying habits?

Some examples might be as follows.

- A woman who is happily married
- A woman who is unhappily married
- A woman who is on her own

Next do the same for a man.

This will give you six potential characters.

Now it's time to have a think about the difference their age would make.

If they were twenty instead of fifty, would they still hold the same views, do the same things?

Once you have a set of stock characters, when you are stuck for an idea for a story, all you have to do is find a situation, funny, sad or scary, put one of them into it, then sit back and see what they do.

This technique can bring life to a story that isn't working as well as it could. All you have to do is remove your main character, and replace them with somebody from your stock list.

As you do more writing, you might want to expand your cast of characters, giving them back stories, endearing and annoying habits, favourite films, books and so on. With any luck, you may find that you get to know one of the characters so well you will want to write a longer story featuring them, maybe even a serial or a novel.

If this all sounds like a lot of work, you can cheat and take a short cut. For a ready made cast of characters, see the entry under *Horoscopes*.

Whichever method you choose, once you have your actors you can cast them in any role you can think of and see how they behave. With any luck, a story will start to emerge.

Christmas and New Year

There is always a big demand for Christmas stories as many magazines have festive specials as well as their regular issues. As with any seasonal story, it's important to start work on your stories early. January is not too soon.

I keep a special drawer in my filing cabinet for Christmas snippets so that when I need to come up with an idea, I have plenty of stimuli to choose from. Into that drawer go Christmas cards, cuttings from newspapers and magazines, stories I enjoyed, stories I didn't enjoy but which might be useful, outlines of any Christmas films I watched, the December and January pictures from last year's calendar, in short anything with a winter or a Christmassy theme.

In December, I watch as many festive programmes and films as I can bear. If any ideas start to form, I make a note of them and put them into my drawer.

When I want to write a seasonal story, I pull out that drawer and immediately, that feeling of Christmas comes back, whether it's thirty degrees Celsius or thirty degrees Fahrenheit outside.

I aim to write at least five Christmas themed stories every year as I know I will stand a good chance of selling at least one of them. I use all kinds of ways to kick start an idea, some of which will be explained in greater detail here.

One of the easiest is to 'borrow' somebody else's idea.

There are many classic Christmas stories – films like *White Christmas, It's a Wonderful Life* and *The Grinch,* to name just a few.

There are also the stories surrounding the nativity, such as the shepherds hearing of the birth, the coming of the three wise men, Mary and Joseph's journey and, on a much darker level, the massacre of the innocents.

All of these can be updated or told in a new and different way.

Think about *A Christmas Carol* for a few moments. There have been so many films made of this story, including *A Muppet Christmas Carol*, as well as versions starring Alistair Sim, Patrick Stewart and Bill Murray. There is even a musical stage version. Each of these is very different but they all come from exactly the same source.

So why not try writing your own version of *A Christmas Carol*, or that other, perennial favourite, *The Wizard of Oz*?

The first thing to do is to jot down an outline of the story as simply and as briefly as you can.

For example, thinking about *The Wizard of Oz*, I might write this. A young girl goes to a strange land and wants to get home. To do this, she needs to find the Wizard. On the way she meets a cowardly lion, a scarecrow who has no heart and a tin man who wants a brain.

After various adventures, they get to meet the Wizard only to find that he's not as powerful as they'd thought. That's when they discover that they don't actually need him because they have found all the things they wanted already. All Dorothy has to do is to click her red shoes and she's back home in Kansas.

Now you have a summary of the plot, all you have to do is start to change things.

First, choose who your main character (Dorothy) is going to be. Next, decide what it is that he or she is lacking. For example, you might choose a divorced woman called Susan who wants to find new friends.

Now decide how she might go about doing this. For example, she could choose the internet (the Wizard) but she's not very computer literate and has to find somebody to help her.

In steps her widowed neighbour who she's always found a bit cold (scarecrow) who helps her find a dating site. Faced with having to write a profile, she contacts an old friend to help her. As it happens, that old friend (the tin man) has lost confidence in their abilities since marrying the wrong man. When the heroine decides to meet one of the men from the dating site, she asks her sister (the lion) to go with her. Her sister has never married and has always been nervous of strangers.

It's up to you what happens next. One or all of them could find they already have what they need, as in the original version of the story, or things could go slightly wrong. You can play with the original plot as much as you like. You should soon find something that resonates with you.

If you have your own favourite Christmas story or film, try this technique on it and see where it takes you.

I have read several stories that took their inspiration directly from the original Christmas story, the nativity. I have shied away from doing this as I wouldn't want to offend anyone, but there are plenty of stories out there that prove it can be done.

If this appeals to you, one way to add your own twist would be to tell the story from the viewpoint of a minor character, for example, a young boy who helps the shepherds, or the wife of the innkeeper who let Mary and Joseph sleep in the stable.

Other places I might start a Christmas story from are presents (who wanted want and why), parties, both standard and fancy dress, cooking and eating Christmas dinner, shopping, welcome and unwelcome house guests, mistletoe and how to avoid being kissed by somebody you find repulsive, daft games like Charades, Christmas TV, the Queen's Speech, Christmas number one singles, and so on.

If none of these work for you, try an internet search of Christmas traditions and customs. You will be amazed at the number and variety of things you find, including some of the weird and wonderful things other nations choose to eat on Christmas morning.

What if a friend invited you to Christmas dinner and instead of turkey, they served up a piece of salted fish?

New Year is another time that is a rich source of traditions and superstitions galore.

One of the most well known of these is the tradition of first footing. Basically this is all about making sure that the right person crosses your threshold first in the New Year. Ideally he should be a dark stranger, bearing various gifts, often a coin, bread, salt and coal, which represent food, warmth and good fortune.

All kinds of rules and regulations govern first footing. For example, the man should not be a doctor, and he definitely must not have eyebrows that meet in the middle.

Tradition also dictates that whoever first foots gets to claim a kiss from the ladies.

The question you might want to ask yourself is this. How does a medical man, with eyebrows that join up, get to kiss the woman he admires?

Comedies

It's not easy to write funny stories which is a shame as many fiction editors (*Woman's Weekly*, *Yours* and so on) love humour.

In my view, the best comedy comes from real people living real lives. This goes some way to explain the lasting popularity of television shows like *Only Fools and Horses*, *My Family* and *The Good Life* – we all have our own particular favourites that we can happily watch over and over again.

Mine are a little more off the wall – *Black Books*, *Red Dwarf* and so on, but all situation comedies are full of easy to borrow ideas for stories.

Why is this? Because comedy comes from conflict, often from characters being thwarted in their ambitions. Think for a moment of poor deluded Hyacinth Bucket in *Keeping Up Appearances* whose efforts to put on airs and graces inevitably end in embarrassment, or *Fawlty Towers* where Basil would be perfectly happy to run a hotel if he didn't have to deal with the staff and the customers.

Comedy also comes from situations that, handled in other ways, would be immensely sad and poignant. For example, in *Steptoe and Son*, Harold longs to find love, and dreams of escaping his life as a rag and bone man, but whenever he tries to break free, his cantankerous father gets in the way.

When you think about it, many comedy shows are actually variations on the same theme. Take *Ever Decreasing Circles*, *Some Mothers Do 'Ave 'Em* and *The Brittas Empire*. These all revolve around hapless people trying to do simple things that prove to be beyond them.

Or *Steptoe and Son* and Carla Lane's *Butterflies*. On the surface, these shows may seem very different, but they both have main characters who dream of escaping their humdrum lives.

Hopefully by now, I will have convinced you that it's acceptable to take the plot of a sitcom and turn it into a short story because this is exactly what I'm suggesting. All you have to do is change things round a bit.

For example, you could replace the rag and bone yard in *Steptoe and Son* with an antiques shop, and turn the main characters into a sister and her much older brother.

Now for an **Exercise**. Make a list of your three favourite situation comedies. Imagine you were pitching the idea for the series and write a short blurb outlining the main characters and their relationship to each other, the setting, and the basic premise.

Can you change something to make a different show? If so, you may have a pilot for a brand new series and at the very least, an idea for a short story.

Creative Writing Exercises

I love these.

For me, there's nothing better than being put on the spot and having to write something, straight from the top of your head. The resulting pieces of prose are often rambling and incomplete, but that doesn't matter. They represent an idea that can be used to produce a story later.

Some writers hate creative writing classes and all that they entail. They don't like having to write to order and hate having to read the results to other members. If this is you, I sympathise.

The fact is, nobody should expect to be able to produce a good, polished piece of prose in a few minutes. I certainly can't do it. Most groups won't mind if you sit out, at least until you feel more comfortable. If that doesn't happen, you might not be in the right group so try to find another one, or even start one of your own.

I have been a member of Leeds Writers' Circle for a couple of years (www.leedswriterscircle.co.uk) Every now and then, they run all day workshops on a Saturday and I go to as many as I possibly can, just to take part in the writing exercises. Even though I suffer from an excess of ideas, I can't resist them.

I love finding out all the different ways that other writers use to generate ideas for their writing. As far as I'm concerned, the more, the merrier.

I'd like to share with you a particular favourite of mine which goes like this.

Exercise

First, you ask everyone in the class to name two things that they love or are passionate about. These can be hobbies or interests, people or causes, but cannot be family members. Each person is then told to choose one of those things and write about it from the point of view of a character who hates it.

So if a member of the class loves golf, they would have to write a convincing piece of prose where the main character wouldn't play golf if you paid them and thinks it's the most boring sport in the world, or as Mark Twain once said, "a good walk spoiled."

This is a great exercise for forcing writers to step outside their comfort zone and get inside a character's head so that they see the world the way the character does.

It helps writers to produce varied characters, rather than people who are simply versions of themselves. It's challenging, but great fun too.

Another **Exercise** I enjoy, because it's all about memory and the meaning attached to otherwise meaningless things, goes like this. Take along a selection of objects and ask people to write about the person they might have belonged to, or any memories of their own that are triggered.

Here it is often the most mundane object that produces the greatest effect, because everybody will have come into contact with something like it before. If you are stuck, try these: a box of matches, a bottle of perfume, a pen, a classic novel, a pair of gloves, a toy car, a ruler, and a safety pin.

When I do this exercise, I encourage people to pick up their chosen object so that they can use all their senses to find out what it feels like or how it smells, as well as what it looks like.

The trick is not to try too hard, just relax and think about your chosen object, letting your thoughts wander where they choose.

You will find lots of exercises dotted throughout this book. My advice is to try them all and see which of them gets the best results.

Cartoon by Tim Bean

Crime

One of the easiest ways to come up with a crime story is to adapt a true story. There are several magazines on the market devoted to this subject, as a trip to any newsagent will prove.

If you shy away from murder and other violent crimes, you might want to think about the cosier side of the genre, as exemplified by Alexander McCall Smith. His stories are often less about the actual crimes and more about the personalities involved.

Start by making a list of as many different crimes as you can think of. Here are a few to get you started.

Shoplifting, fraud, blackmail, kidnap, extortion, mugging, burglary, grievous bodily harm, poison pen letters, murder.

Once you have the list, ask yourself which crime(s) you know most about, or are more interested in. These are the ones it's probably best to work with first.

Now whenever you read a newspaper, watch out for any stories involving that particular crime and start to build up a file. Again, the internet can be very useful.

Murder usually tops the list. Human beings have always been fascinated by the subject, but take care when using murder as a theme for a short story. It's very hard to do successfully. In order to understand why a person is driven to murder, we need to know them very well and there usually isn't the room in a short story to explore this.

Sadly, editors have seen far too many stories where a man murders his wife and buries her body in the rose bed. Poisoned mushrooms have also been done to death (sorry about the pun). So if you do fancy writing about murder, you will need to be more original. That said, you can sometimes disguise a lack of originality by injecting some humour.

I tried the following story on several UK magazines with no luck. It was eventually published in Scandinavia and also appears in the short story collection, *Crime Shorts Too*.

Not on the Same Wavelength

Beverley glared across the room at Howard as he sat, head buried in the Sunday papers. What had happened to the man she'd fallen in love with? What happened to the man who made her laugh, the man who could almost read her mind?

They used to be able to finish each other's sentences. She still could sometimes, but not because they were on the same wavelength, it was because their dialogue had shrunk so much in recent years. Now their conversations rarely went beyond a few much repeated phrases.

As she looked at him, she recognised her feelings for what they were - hate.

It had been months since they made love and weeks since they'd had a decent conversation. All those sweet endearing habits that she used to find so appealing now irritated her beyond measure. The way he never put the milk back in the fridge after making coffee, the way he left the washing-up in the sink, his toothy smile. Everything.

Opposites attract, the saying went, and so they did, at first. Now the differences between them stretched chasm wide.

"I want a divorce." The sound of her voice surprised her, she hadn't meant to say the words out loud.

"What's that you say, dear?"

She frowned at him. His slight deafness was another thing she used to find sweet, but which now drove her mad. "I want a divorce," she repeated.

"Don't be silly, Beverley. That would mean selling the house. You don't want that, do you?" and he disappeared back behind the paper.

She felt like snatching the paper away and hitting him over the head with it, or better still, hitting him with a lamp or even a chair. She was so fed up with all the arguments and squabbles, but he was right about one thing. A divorce wasn't the ideal solution. The house meant more to her than Howard did, and she was sure he felt the same way. Neither of them would want to lose it.

There was only one thing she could do - murder him.

It was amazing how much better she felt once she'd made up her mind. She had something to think about, something to plan. It made putting up with his irritating ways so much easier.

Now as she looked at his balding head, all she needed to do was imagine him dead. She smiled to herself. It was lucky they were no longer on the same wavelength. The last thing she wanted was for him to know what she was thinking.

She began visiting the library as often as she could, reading crime novels, searching for a foolproof plan. The killing part was easy enough. The difficult bit was getting away with it. Shooting and stabbing were both too messy and however much she hated Howard, she wasn't sure she had the courage to spill his blood herself.

Hiring an assassin would have been ideal if she'd had known how to go about it. Unfortunately, there was no listing in the telephone book for hired killers. Fixing the car was no good either; firstly because she had no idea what was involved. and secondly, Howard rarely went above forty miles an hour, even when he drove her Mercedes.

She was left with just two options - arranging some kind of accident, or using poison. Despite reading countless novels, several months passed and she was no nearer a solution, then one day, when she wasn't even looking for the answer, it came to her.

She was flicking through her favourite cookery book when she noticed a recipe for mushroom soup. At the bottom of the page was a warning.

'Some mushrooms are extremely poisonous. If picking wild mushrooms, always seek expert advice.'

That was it! The answer was there all the time.

She started to read up on the subject. There were several kinds of mushrooms that could make people ill, but very few that would prove fatal. In the end, it came down to just one particular kind - the only one that grew near in the nearby woods.

Unfortunately, they only occurred at certain times of the year. It meant she had several months to wait, but she didn't mind. She could use the time to lull Howard into a false sense of security.

She took to walking in the woods, looking for and identifying mushrooms, until she was confident she knew which were fine to eat and which were not. The last thing she wanted was to raise her husband's suspicions by accidentally giving him a stomach upset. Her plan needed to be foolproof.

That day, she made her first batch of soup.

She watched as Howard polished off a bowlful.

"Delicious," he said, "and free too."

She managed not to frown. Soon she wouldn't have to put up with his penny-pinching ways any longer.

From that day on, she picked mushrooms at least once a week, and turned them into soup. Each time she served it, she looked forward to the day when Howard's bowl would have an extra, special ingredient - a deadly poisonous mushroom. That would soon wipe the smile off his face.

As the weeks passed, she found it increasingly hard to be patient. Luckily, Howard had started to spend more time in the garage, tuning, polishing and customising his precious camper van. In the old days, she would have felt jealous and neglected, now she was just glad he was out of the way.

At last, the day came when she found what she'd been waiting for. She stared at the tiny mushroom. It was hard to imagine that something so beautiful and so small could kill a fully grown man.

Carefully, reverently even, she knelt down and gently picked the mushroom, placing it in a separate paper bag, well away from the other mushrooms she'd already gathered.

Back home, she made two portions of soup - one deadly, and one harmless.

That evening, it was hard not to smile as she watched Howard eating the poisonous soup.

"That was excellent. Very tasty," he said as he emptied the bowl.

She almost felt sorry for the stupid fool. If the books she'd read were to be believed, he'd be dead by morning.

"I said I'd go round to my sister's this evening. She's feeling lonely with Tom working away."

"Do you want me to come with you?" asked Howard.

"There's no need. I thought I might stay the night. It will cheer her up."

She knew Howard wouldn't object. It wasn't as though her absence from the marriage bed made a difference any more. She called her sister to confirm the arrangements, packed a small case and left the house.

As she stepped out into the crisp early evening air, she took a deep breath. Just one more day and she'd be free.

She got into her car and adjusted the seat. Every time Howard drove the Mercedes, he never put the seat back in the right position. It was just one of the many things that annoyed her about him, but not for much longer, she thought.

She pulled her mirror from her bag and practised pulling a sad face.

"I've been picking mushrooms for months now. I had no idea they could be so poisonous. Howard loved my homemade soups," she spoke the words out loud, as if she was on the stage. Acting the part of the grieving widow was a role she could hardly wait to play.

She started the engine and drove away, turning off the main road and onto the motorway.

The Mercedes was her car, chosen for its good looks and for its speed. Driving fast exhilarated her, and as the car reached 85 miles per hour, she felt so good, she started singing along with the radio.

From now on, she could do whatever she liked.

She wound down the window, letting in a blast of cold air. Howard always drove with the heater on, and the radio off. Well now, she could do what SHE wanted for a change.

She pushed the car to go faster, enjoying the feeling of excitement it gave her, but then the car in front braked suddenly. Beverley slammed her foot down on the brakes, but nothing happened. When she tried again, the pedal came away. In desperation she swerved, trying to steer the car out of danger, but it was no good, she was going much too fast. The car veered off the road at high speed.

She knew at once that this was her husband's doing.

Those long hours spent in the garage had obviously been used to find ways to fix her car. All the time she'd been trying to find a foolproof way to murder him, he'd been doing exactly the same thing.

Her dying thought made her smile.

She'd been wrong about Howard. It seemed they were still on the same wavelength after all.

As you can see, this story uses not just one tired cliché, but several — mushrooms, tampering with the brakes, and murdering a spouse — and I still managed to find a home for it.

All of which goes to prove two things. Firstly, there are rules, but there's nothing to stop you breaking them and secondly, and most importantly, ideas can be used over and over again.

Dates and Anniversaries

There are certain dates that mean something to everybody – December 25th, January 1st, February 14th, October 31st and November 5th, to name just a few.

Each one conjures up its own atmosphere and because we all know what happens on these dates, a reader will already have some idea what to expect. For example, if a story centres around January 1st, they might expect cold weather and much talk of resolutions.

Expectations are great because you can either play along with them or you can subvert them (for example, by setting the story in Australia where January will be warm and sunny).

It also gives you an ideal opportunity to play with your cast of ready-made characters. All you have to do is choose a date, select one of them and see what they do.

For example, a forty year old woman who is happily married would have a very different Valentine's Day to a woman who was on her own.

Other dates are less obvious but can also be useful for conjuring up ideas. For example, Saint's Days, Easter, Thanksgiving, the day the clocks go forward and back, Twelfth Night.

The other great thing about dates is that fiction editors often like to feature stories that are relevant to the season and/or are topical, even going so far as running themed issues around them. Using stories based around a set time of year help to make the magazine feel bang up to date (which is why stories about snow and ice tend to appear in the winter, and holiday stories in the summer).

Anniversaries also make good starting points. These can be anniversaries of famous people's births or death, anniversaries of battles or when something significant happened (e.g. the first colour TV broadcast, or the first ascent of Mount Everest).

For an endless supply of these, all you need to do is an internet search along the lines of anniversaries in June 2012, or what happened (insert number) years ago. Once you find something that interests you, you can decide what kind of story you want to write.

For example, if the event happened a hundred years ago you might want to set your story in those times, or you might choose to write from the point of view of a ghost who was alive then. Or you can set the story in the present day asking yourself why that particular anniversary could be important to someone.

If an event proves particularly interesting, you might want to take a break from fiction and pitch an article instead. Either way, dates and anniversaries are a fresh and constantly changing source of ideas.

Wedding anniversaries are also worth a mention here. For some reason, different anniversaries are associated with different materials. For example, year one is paper or cotton, year five is wood, and year ten is tin. How happy a woman would be if her husband gave her a tin of baked beans as an anniversary present, I don't know, but I'm sure that has the makings of a short story.

Not all anniversaries mark happy occasions. You might want to think about somebody whose spouse died five years ago and how that might make them feel. Take care not to make any assumptions here. Assumptions are things we want readers to make. As writers we can be far more devious. For example, the woman might be glad her husband died.

See separate entries for *Halloween, November 5th*, and *Valentine's Day*.

Dates, Other

There are other dates to think about too – first dates, blind dates.

Have a think back to some of yours. What do you remember? Did they work out well or end in tears? Were you ever stood up? If so, how did that make you feel? Did you put on a brave face, or cry enough tears to fill a cup?

Again, why not take one of your stock characters and see how they cope on a first date. For example, how would a seventy year old be feeling when facing their first date for more than forty years? Rather differently from a fifteen year old, that's for certain.

Imagine you had known somebody for a number of years. Maybe they've asked you out before and you've said no because you weren't attracted to them, but now something has changed the way you feel. Or you were in a relationship which has now ended, and you would like to get to know them better. How would you go about it?

Would you even dare to do it? If the person says no, your friendship could be permanently damaged. This was the predicament raised in the hit film, *When Harry Met Sally*.

Think about this problem for a while. What would you do, and why? Try the same question with one of your stock characters.

Now take a step back and introduce a third person. What if that person knew this couple and was sure they were meant to be together, but neither of them is willing to make the first move. What could they do to push them together?

I have always found this line of questioning very productive. It has led me to several stories that went on to be published, so it's worth spending some time on.

If you are stuck, try these for size.

- You could send the person on an errand where they will meet the potential date.
- Send them both Valentine's cards, signed with the appropriate initials.
- Invite one round when you know the other person will be dropping in.
- Arrange to go to the theatre with one of the people, then make an excuse and cancel, offering the other person the spare ticket.

I'm sure you can think of plenty of others. Now all you have to do is decide what happens at the end.

Another useful date that comes round at least a couple of times a year is Friday the thirteenth. Is that a day when your main character prefers to stay home, tucked up in bed? If so, what happens when they are invited to an interview on that day?

It just so happened that when I went on *The Weakest Link*, the filming took place on Friday the thirteenth. I knew it had to be lucky for one of the team.

I was right. I came away as the strongest link and with a cheque for £1,350.

Events

Events are often date specific, which makes them topical and therefore appealing to editors.

Often these are sporting events, which will be looked at in the next section. Others include anniversaries of famous people's births or deaths and special occasions, such as the Queen's Jubilee. There are also anniversaries of battles, wars, and other important events, which can all make the basis of a short story.

I wrote one for the two hundredth anniversary of Isambard Kingdom Brunel's birth, which happened in 2006.

Instead of writing something historical, I chose to write about a long suffering wife who accompanied her husband, a huge fan of steam trains and in particular of Brunel, on a special trip to mark the anniversary.

I could have written the story from the husband's point of view, as it was his interest in Brunel that sparked the story idea, but I chose to do something that bit different and made the sale.

Local research can also come in handy here. Are there any carnivals or parades, music festivals or other celebrations that take place near to where you live? If so, why not go along and soak up the atmosphere.

Exercise

Find an event that's due to happen in six months' time and do some research around it.

Now think of somebody who might be interested in marking that event and how they might want to go about it.

Next, add another character, either a parent or partner of the first character, who has no interest whatsoever in that event.

What happens? Do they both end up happy or disappointed? Or does just one of them get their own way?

When using dates and events as a basis for a story, it's important to bear in mind the timescales involved in putting a magazine together. In other words, makes sure that you don't send the piece at the wrong time.

Submitting something too early is much better than too late.

Events, Sporting and Other

Sport is big business.

Hardly a day goes by when some kind of sport doesn't feature on the main television channels.

Many of these have major events attached to them. These can be big, international, occasions like the World Cup or the Olympics which only come round every four years, or ones that happen every year like Wimbledon or the FA Cup. There are many more. The Derby, the Grand National, the Oxford and Cambridge Boat Race, Formula One, the Open Golf Championship, and World Snooker are just some I could mention.

Have you been to any of these? If you have, think back and see if you have a ready made story there. Alternatively, imagine a character, either one of your stock group, yourself, or somebody completely different, and put them at the event. Then ask the usual questions – why are they there, who are they with? Are they enjoying themselves or not?

Now start to think about other people your character can see, people who may not be there to watch the action, people like cleaners, ticket sellers, catering staff, and so on. What does the event mean to them? More money, more work maybe.

Exercise

Try making a small mind map, putting the sporting event in the middle, then branching out to the various people who could be involved. Now pick one of those people and tell the story of their day, drip feeding in small clues about the sporting event, but don't reveal what it is until the end.

If you find this difficult, why not think of how a criminal might use a sporting event to their advantage? Some possibilities appear at the end of this section.

Of course, there are plenty more sporting events that don't make the newspapers or get shown on television.

I'm thinking here of fun runs, sponsored swims and so on that are held to raise money for charity. These make very fertile ground for ideas. All you do is, yes, you've guessed it, ask the right questions. I suggest starting with why the person is taking part.

Make a list of all the reasons you can think of as to why somebody might take part in a sponsored sport event. If you struggle with this, glance at the end of this section for some possible answers.

You will see that the reasons people do things can be many and varied. Just because the event is for charity doesn't mean that people will, necessarily, be taking part for charitable reasons.

There are also some very strange 'sporting' events that take place up and down the country. Cheese rolling, shin kicking, toe wrestling and pancake races are just a few examples. If you choose one of these to write a story round, people can hardly help but be interested. If I saw that a story was about worm charming or snail racing, I would HAVE to read it.

As always, details of all kinds of strange sports that take place in Britain today can be found in minutes using the internet.

As with major sporting events, thinking about characters not directly involved in the sport can produce good results. I would love to read about the wife of a man whose hobby is racing snails. How does she feel about it? Do the snails live in the house? Does her husband have a favourite? If he does, is his wife jealous of it?

74

I can already feel the threads of an idea coming together, but I'm not going to write the story. That's your job.

Reasons somebody might take part in a sponsored event

Here are some reasons that are linked to the charity.

The person suffered from cancer and are now well, they have just found out that they have the disease, they lost somebody dear to them, or they work for the charity.

Now for some reasons that aren't quite so charitable.

- Somebody dared them to take part.
- They have been trying to get fit and the event is a good way to test their fitness levels.
- They want to impress their boss, their family, their friends, or a potential partner.
- A rival is taking part and they are determined to beat them.

Of course, there may be darker motives.

Staying with the sponsored event, the person may be keeping most of the money for themselves.

If the event involves swimming, a criminal might try to steal other people's possessions when they get changed.

A pickpocket would look forward to an FA Cup Final match, or any event where crowds are likely to gather. Crowds also make it easier for kidnappers to pounce, or for a murderer to kill their victim. With all the noise that goes on at a football match, people would be less likely to hear somebody's calls for help, even screams might go unnoticed.

Criminals could also print fake tickets and sell them at elevated prices.

Any of these would work as a short story. All you have to do is begin by making it seem that the criminal is just a fan, supporting their local team or enjoying an evening out, then turn the whole thing on its head when their true nature becomes clear.

Fairy Tales

Ever since mankind first learned how to talk, we have been telling each other stories.

Some of those early works of fiction are still with us in the form of myths, legends, and fairy tales.

When we think of fairy tales, we often think of Hans Christian Anderson or the Brothers Grimm, but most of the stories they tell have their origins further back in history.

In many cases, it's almost as though they've been around forever, which means that writers can happily steal the plots for their own devious purposes.

This is great fun to do, firstly because there is a ready-made plot and secondly, these stories are populated by a whole host of fascinating characters that the vast majority of people are already aware of.

That fact makes it so much easier to make the characters sympathetic because readers already understand how they tick before you've even written a sentence.

There are all kinds of ways to use fairy tales to generate new story ideas. You can tell the story in exactly the same way, and simply update it to the present day.

You could change the ending, making it sad instead of happy, or as is often the case in traditional fairy tales, happy instead of sad. For a good example of a sad ending, try reading the original story of *The Little Mermaid* – it's horrifying.

My favourite method is to ignore the usual hero or heroine and focus the action on another character entirely.

For example, I took the story of *Cinderella* and instead of looking at things from her point of view, I chose to let one of the ugly sisters tell the story using entries from her diary.

To make things more interesting, I also updated the story, turning Prince Charming into Prince William – this was before he was married!

If you want to read the story, it's included in the collection *Alternative Renditions*, which was published by Bridge House.

Another method you can use to shake things up is to tell the story in a totally different way.

Another one of my rewritten fairy tales is called *Modern Times*.

This is an updated version of a well known fairy tale (in this case, *Snow White*) with the additional twist of being told in epistolary fashion. That means it's written in the form of a series of letters, the method Bram Stoker used in *Dracula*.

I've included the story here so you can see how closely (or not) it sticks to the original fairy tale.

MODERN TIMES

To whom it may concern
Social Services Department.
1ˢᵗ February
Dear Sirs
I'm worried about my neighbours. They're all very old and have nobody to take care of them.

Could somebody call on them and make sure they're OK? I would do it myself, but I'm eighty one. I can hardly manage my own housework.
Their address is Cavern Cottage at the end of Cherry Tree Lane.
Yours, a worried neighbour
Letitia Hartley (Mrs).

16th March
Dear Mrs Hartley
Thank you for your letter.
Regretfully, this Department is unable to comply with your request. The said party has not requested a domiciliary visit and we therefore cannot execute any formal proceedings.
Yours faithfully,
Germaine Garson (Ms)

19th March
Dear Ms Garson
Since I first wrote to you, my neighbours' condition has worsened.
One of them has a permanent bad cold. Another is definitely several apples short of a pie and would benefit from day care or occupational therapy. They could all benefit from meals on wheels or at least a home help.
Yours truly,
Letitia Hartley

25th April
Dear Mrs Hartley
Ms Garson has taken maternity leave as her partner, Jemima, has just given birth to triplets. Your correspondence has been passed to me.
We cannot interfere unless requested to do so by the parties concerned as this would contravene European Union edict number 567,456,234A.
Yours truly,
Sid Greene (Ms)

29th April

Dear Ms Greene

Your letter infuriated me. My neighbours were miners until they retired. Even now, they work hard, digging on their allotments.

Fortunately you need concern yourselves no longer. A teenage girl has moved in with them.

She's a lovely little thing. Of course, I say little, but she's taller than any of the old men.

Apparently she ran away from her stepmother and my neighbours have offered her free board for as long as she wants. In return, she takes care of the house. I thought I should let you know so that you can close your file.

Yours truly,

Letitia Hartley

1st May

Dear Mrs Hartley

The department has taken immediate action to investigate this worrying situation. A young girl, living with seven vertically challenged dirty old men is exactly the kind of unsavoury domestic arrangement that cannot be allowed to continue.

Our investigator paid a visit, and spoke to two of the men. One blushed whenever my colleague mentioned the young girl, (they call her Snow White!), and his friend kept smirking at my colleague in a most disconcerting manner.

My department has managed to locate the girl's stepmother, Mrs W.I. Kidd, and she is coming down on Monday the 5th of May to collect her.

Thank you for bringing this sordid matter to our attention.

Yours truly,

Portia Blakestaff (Ms),

Family Values Consultant

5th May

Dear Ms Blakestaff

When I got your letter, I rushed round to see Snow White. The poor girl is terrified of her stepmother. Luckily, I was there when the wicked woman arrived.

She was nowhere near as lovely as Snow White who is without doubt one of the fairest girls in all the land.

I stayed in the room, in case she tried anything. When she saw that I wasn't going to leave them alone, she finally got up to go. As she left, she gave Snow White an apple.

I didn't think there could be any harm in a bright shiny Golden Delicious but the moment Snow White bit into it she fell, dead, on the floor.

The dwarfs were so upset, even Happy cried buckets.

They laid her body on the sofa. She looked so beautiful. It's such a terrible waste.

I hope your Department is pleased with itself. You have caused the death of an innocent young girl.

Yours faithfully,

Letitia Hartley

7th May

Without prejudice

Dear Mrs Hartley

The Department wishes to make it clear that we take no responsibility for anything that happens as a result of our intervention in what was purely a domestic matter.

Yours truly,

Martha J. Prendergast B.A.

Senior Legal Executive

12th May

Dear Ms Blakestaff et al,

I am writing to tell you how things turned out with Snow White..

The dwarfs were too upset to do anything practical so I got in touch with Palace and Prince Funeral Directors on their behalf.

Young Mr William Prince came round - a most charming young man. The moment he saw Snow White, he fell hopelessly in love.

It was heartbreaking to see. He went over to her, tears pouring down his face, and kissed her poor dead lips.

Then, as he and his colleague moved her body outside to the waiting hearse, Dopey managed to trip over Sleepy, who was snoozing on the rug as usual.

Mr Prince was knocked right off his feet and Snow White fell to the ground. As she hit the floor, a piece of apple flew out of her mouth. It was like a miracle. She just coughed, and sat up, good as new, as if nothing had happened.

She looked at William, and he looked at her, and you could tell they were going to be in love forever and a day. It was like a fairy tale come true.

I would like to thank you all.

If it wasn't for your department's incompetence, Snow White would never have met her Prince. As it is, they're to be married as soon as she is sixteen. Meanwhile, the dwarfs have asked me to act as her godmother, a role I am very happy to play.

Yours truly,

Mrs Letitia Hartley

17ᵗʰ June

Dear Mrs Hartley

Upon reading your file I think you may be suffering from some form of dementia and have asked the departmental psychiatrist, Dr. H. Von Rumplestiltzkin to call on you as soon as possible.

Try to stay calm. Your delusions are not real. Everybody knows that in these modern times, there are no such things as fairy tales.

Yours truly,

Mr Jakob Grimm

Head of Psychiatric Social Services.

As you can see, the basic plot follows the original fairy tale quite closely, keeping many of the original characters.

This story is a favourite of mine because it was such fun to write. It has had quite an interesting life.

When I first wrote it, it was two thousand words long and was submitted to *Woman's Weekly*. After they rejected it, it went the rounds of the other magazines I hoped might want to buy it. None of them did, but a lady at my writers' club liked the story and encouraged me to send it to a competition.

There was a problem though.

Entries had to be a maximum of one thousand words. Undeterred, I cut the story down until it met the required word count then sent it off. I'm happy to say that it won the £200 first prize.

Some time later, Bridge House were calling for updated fairy tales for a new collection. This time, stories needed to be three thousand words long. So I took the original two thousand word version and padded it out until I had a longer version.

The competition winning, one thousand word version is the one that is included here.

In my opinion, the original version, which nobody wanted, is the best but what do I know?

So back to fairy tales and another **Exercise**.

Make a list of all the fairy tales you know well (think of pantomimes or try an internet search if you are stuck).

Choose the one you know best, or the one you like the most, then pick one of the minor characters as your hero or heroine.

Now ask yourself those all important questions by imagining that you are interviewing them for a newspaper article. What do they think about the hero or heroine? What's their angle on the story? Does their involvement change everything, or does the story still end in exactly the same way, despite their best efforts?

To get you started, here are a few suggestions.

Think about Buttons from the pantomime version of *Cinderella*. I always feel sorry for him. We all know he loves the girl, so can you find a way to help him win her?

Or maybe *Hansel and Gretel* could be made more interesting for a modern day audience by telling the witch's story instead. If you gave her a troubled background, you might be able to make her sympathetic.

Then there's the genie from *Aladdin*. Have you ever thought what his life must be like, cooped up in that lamp for centuries, waiting for some greedy person to summon him?

If that was me, when I came out, I'd be more than grumpy.

Another way to extract ideas from fairy tales is to change the disposition of the main character.

For example, what if *Cinderella* was actually rather vain and lazy and made Buttons do all the work? Or taking the same fairy tale, what if the wicked stepmother was really kind and considerate and it was her daughters who were the real villains?

If you try this technique on your favourite story, you can't help but generate some good, original, ideas. You could even copy my idea and tell a story in a series of letters (or emails).

Fears and Phobias

Most people, I'd say all but there's bound to be an exception somewhere, are frightened of something that other people don't find in the least bit scary. My weakness is crane flies, also known as Daddy Longlegs. I can't stand them.

Some popular phobias are fear of spiders (arachnophobia), enclosed spaces (claustrophobia), heights (acrophobia) and open spaces (agoraphobia). Sufferers from any of these face problems in their day to day lives that other people can scarcely imagine.

As problems are the life blood of fiction, a story where a character has to face their fear in some way could be a good starting point.

Do you have any phobias? If you do, think back to a time when it caused you a problem. How did you cope? How did the people with you react? Is there a ready-made story there?

What if your main character is phobic about cats, then falls in love with a woman who owns six of them?

What is he going to do about it? Will he overcome his fear, or lose the love of his life? Will his paramour sacrifice her pets? Will they find another way to get round the problem?

As always, a quick search on the internet will reveal an amazing number of phobias.

It turns out that people can be afraid of almost anything. There are hundreds of phobias to choose from which means hundreds of potential storylines.

Here's one of mine based around the fear of flying.

A WING AND A PRAYER

Brian did up his seat belt. In just under an hour and a half, he'd be in Scotland with his family. He pulled out his newspaper and pretended to read. With luck, whoever sat next to him would get the message he didn't want to talk. Just then, a middle aged woman plonked a bag down on the empty seat.

Brian ignored her as she put a coat and goodness knows what else up on the shelf. He noticed she was wearing perfume. He sniffed a little huffily, his late wife only wore perfume in the evenings. To his dismay, as soon as the woman was settled she leaned towards him and held out a hand in greeting. Politeness forced him to take it.

"I'm Marion. Marion Haynes. Looks like we're stuck with each other for the next hour or so."

"Brian Mannerton," he said as he shook the offered hand, then he nodded in what he hoped was a suitably dismissive way, and flapped his newspaper open.

The woman kept fidgeting, reaching down into her bag, taking out sweets and a variety of papers. He wondered what she was doing. Didn't she know that bags had to be put away during take-off? He bit his lip. He didn't want a conversation.

Just then the engines started and the plane taxied towards the runway. Marion became still, too still. He risked a quick glance. Her head was pushed back hard against the seat, and her eyes were tightly closed. He took a longer look and saw that her knuckles were white from where she was gripping the arm rests and her lips were moving in silent prayer.

"Are you OK?" he asked. Just then the plane's speed increased as it began to hurtle along the runway.

She nodded stiffly, keeping her eyes tightly shut. "I'm terrified of flying," she muttered through clenched teeth.

"Is this your first time?" he asked her.

She shook her head violently and braced every muscle in her body for the take-off. Only when they were safely up did she relax her grip and open her eyes.

"That's the worst part over." She managed a wan smile. "You'd think I'd have got used to it by now."

"Why do you fly, if it scares you so much?"

"It's the easiest way to travel. Besides, in Australia you don't have much choice." Now the anxiety had faded from her voice, Brian noticed the mildest of accents.

He turned back to his paper, but he couldn't concentrate, it was as though he could feel Marion's nerves, screaming at him. It was no use. He'd have to try and help her.

"Flying's very safe these days. If you believe the statistics," he said.

"I know," she agreed. "My problem is, however hard I try, I just can't understand how something as enormous as this stays up in the air."

"It's all about lift and drag," said Brian. "Air currents, shape of the wing. That kind of thing."

"So I'm told, but however many times it's explained to me, I still don't understand it."

Brian laughed, then bent down and pulled a book out of his hand luggage. "I've got just what you need," he said as he handed it to her.

The cover featured a cartoon helicopter. She checked the back. "But this book is for children."

"It belongs to my grandson, Charlie. He's six. Take a look at page five. It explains how an aircraft takes off."

She turned the pages. "There are an awful lot of pictures," she said

"Read it. You'll be glad you did. I promise."

A couple of minutes later, she lifted her head and smiled at him. "OK, it makes taking off easy to understand, but how about staying up here? Can it explain that?"

He turned over the pages. "There," he said.

"Good grief," she said as she read. "What an amazing book! It makes everything sound so easy."

"Told you," he said just as the drinks trolley appeared alongside.

"I feel so much better after reading that," she said. "Let me get you a drink."

A whisky sprang to mind, but he thought Marion might not approve. "Thanks. Just a coffee."

"Make that two," she told the stewardess. "I thought I'd need a stiff drink, to steady my nerves, but thanks to you, I don't need it," she said as she passed him his cup. "Are you going to Edinburgh on business?"

Brian shook his head. "No. I took early retirement last year. Now I work part-time, compiling crosswords and puzzles for magazines."

"Wow! That sounds clever."

"Not really," he laughed. "But I enjoy it. I'm visiting my daughter Sheila and her family." He sipped his drink. "My wife and I used to drive up here from Devon, every year. There weren't any direct flights back then."

"Been on your own long?"

"Four years. How about you?"

She nodded. "I moved to Australia twenty-two years ago when I got married. I loved it there, but the minute Mark died, I couldn't wait to get back to England. I came back six months ago, got myself a place just outside Totnes. Do you know it?"

"Know it! I live in Torquay. We're practically neighbours."

"Small world, isn't it?" And she told him about the store she helped run in Queensland, and her part-time career as an actress. "First thing I did when I got back to England was join the nearest Amateur Dramatics Society."

"So why are you going to Scotland?"

"My grandparents came from Edinburgh and I've never been there. I thought it was time I put that right."

As they chatted, Brian lost track of time. He was surprised when the captain announced they were coming in to land.

"Hold my hand until we're down, would you? Just in case I get scared again."

"My pleasure," he said.

"So, safe and sound at last," she said as they touched down. "Look, I hope you don't think it's forward of me, but do you fancy getting together sometime? I'll be home in about two weeks." She wrote her number down and gave it to him.

"Sure. I'd love to," he said as he slipped the paper into his pocket.

"Don't forget to call me," she said as they made their way out of the airport. "Talking to you made me forget all about being frightened."

Then as she turned towards the taxi rank, she gave him a huge wink. Suddenly the penny dropped. Brian realised it had all been an act. Marion wasn't afraid of flying, not in the least.

"Granddad!" shouted a small excited voice.

He walked briskly towards his family and scooped his grandson up into his arms.

"How was it, Dad?" asked Sheila. "It's not easy flying for the first time."

"It wasn't as bad as I thought," he said, returning the boy to the ground.

"Did you read my book, Granddad?" asked Charlie.

Brian laughed. "At least twenty-five times. It was a great help. More than you could ever know." He turned just in time to see Marion disappear into a cab. He grinned, then followed his daughter out to the car park.

Marion didn't know it yet but she wasn't the only one who'd been pretending. Brian had been pretending too; pretending to be calm when in reality he'd been scared to death. That's why Charlie had sent him his book.

He wondered what she would say when he told her. One thing was certain, he could hardly wait to find out.

As you can see, this story is all about people pretending to be something they are not.

The woman pretends to be scared and the hero pretends not to be.

All you have to do is apply this same idea to other phobias and you have a story.

For example, somebody could pretend to be afraid of thunder so that she can shelter with a neighbour who they secretly fancy. You could do the same with spiders and all kinds of other things.

Films

Do you have a favourite film, one you can watch over and over again? If so, have you ever thought about stealing the plot and using it in a short story? I know I have.

One of my favourites is *It's a Wonderful Life*. You probably know the storyline, but in case you don't, this is how it goes. Basically, it's a feel-good Christmas film where James Stewart stars as the good guy George, who runs a building society.

When things go wrong, he blames himself. He's about to throw himself off a bridge when a probationary angel intervenes. The angel, whose name is Clarence, shows our hero what would have happened to the people he loves if he hadn't been there. After seeing these visions, George finds new strength, and goes back to sort out his problems, and it all ends happily.

My story is rather more domestic.

Like the original, mine is set at Christmas. The main character is a put-upon woman whose family have come to stay for the holidays. They are treating her like a slave. Pushed beyond endurance, she runs out of the house and meets an angel. As with the original film, the angel shows the woman what her family's lives would be like if she hadn't been there to help and look after them.

He does this expecting her to go back home and carry on with her life, but she does something else entirely.

If you want to read my version of the story, you can find it in another Bridge House collection entitled *Making Changes* as well as in my own collection of short stories, *Twisting the Night Away*.

Films can be used for ideas in the same way as fairy tales. You can change all kinds of things from the ending to who the main character is. Next time you settle down to watch a film at home (the cinema will probably be too dark), have a notebook ready to jot down anything that grabs your attention. This might be a line of dialogue, a setting, or an interesting minor character whose story could be developed.

Again, keep asking lots of questions. For example, what difference would it make if the story was told from somebody else's point of view?

Film titles can also be used to kick-start an idea.

When doing this, it helps not to think of the actual film. Instead, allow your mind to roam free.

For example, *Gone With The Wind* is a classic love story set against the backdrop of the American Civil War, but what else could it be? You could try a mind map here or just think laterally and ask those all important questions.

What could be 'gone with the wind'?

The story could be about somebody's shed being damaged in a storm, or it might be about a woman who feels she has wasted her life, never having followed her dream, let alone chased it. When she sees the wind scooping up the autumn leaves, it forces her to take stock of her life. What happens next is up to you.

Romantic comedies, otherwise known as romcoms, are some of my favourites to take inspiration from as they're all about relationships.

10 Things I Hate About You, starring the late Heath Ledger, succeeds as well as it does thanks to the lively interplay between the characters. Not only that, the film is a perfect example of a stolen plot.

The story line was taken directly from Shakespeare's *The Taming of the Shrew* and goes something like this – the hero's friend can't take the younger sister to the prom until the older sister (the shrew) also has a date.

If romantic comedies aren't your cup of tea, don't worry, because any kind of film will do.

For example, think of your favourite science fiction film. I have so many of these, but will choose *ET* for the purposes of this exercise. The story is about a boy who meets and befriends an alien.

If I wanted to take this idea and write a story aimed at a women's magazine, I'd probably need to lose the sci-fi angle, so I'd think about that alien and what he represents.

What is ET's actual problem? He's lost and wants to go home.

It's all about not fitting in and the importance of family, home and friendship, which means that your new version of *ET* doesn't need to feature an alien. All you need is a character who is different in some way. In a non sci-fi version, he could follow another religion, or have some kind of disability.

The great thing is that you don't even have to watch a film to use this technique. Newspapers often carry reviews of newly released films, and listing magazines such as *The Radio Times* cover those that are being shown on television.

These reviews are like the blurbs we looked at earlier. They are designed to tell people what the film is about without giving away the whole plot. That means they make ideal starting points for ideas. All you have to do is find one that interests you and carry on with the story.

In my bookcase, I have a copy of *Halliwell's Film Guide* (other people, for example *Virgin* and *The Radio Times*, produce similar guides). A quick browse through the guide helps to remind me of the sheer variety of stories there are available – horror, westerns, spy films, romantic comedies and so on (as I wrote that list, I found myself wondering if I should try a romantic western for a change).

I mainly use the guide to read the descriptions of the films and see if any of them start to make any connections in my mind. This, for example, is what the guide says about *Groundhog Day*.

'A cynical weatherman.....finds himself reliving his day over and over again.....'

What a wonderful idea! All we have to do is change the main character, giving him or her another occupation, then change the setting (maybe even the period the story was set) and you have a brand new story.

Maybe you're thinking, hold on a moment. Everyone will know that it's based on *Groundhog Day*. They will, but that really doesn't matter. Think of *West Side Story*. It's taken directly from *Romeo and Juliet* but that hasn't prevented it from becoming one of the most popular films of all time.

This blurb comes from a film I've neither seen nor heard of before.

'A bored man and wife go their separate ways but are eventually reconciled.'

It's like a miniature story and there are literally thousands to choose from.

The even better news is this – you can buy one of these film guides, second hand, very cheaply (on eBay, for example) as you don't need an up to date edition.

First Lines

First lines are a wonderful starting point for ideas, especially those found in short stories. Why? Because the writer has already done the hard work and produced that all important opening line. You know it did the trick, because the story has been published.

Obviously, you can't copy the story word for word and just change the ending – that would be plagiarism – but there's nothing to stop you using the first line and seeing it where it takes you.

I recommend not reading the stories before you do this exercise. Once you know how they pan out, that's likely to affect your own thoughts. You're using the opening line as a jumping off point to a totally different story, not rewriting the one that's in front of you.

Here are a few from a randomly selected copy of a popular women's magazine.

'Annie parked her car between a Mercedes and a Jaguar.'

'I can read Steven like a book.'

'It all started when I went to pick up the dog from the vet.'

'Yesterday I made a pavlova.'

'Sandra Roberts liked being invisible.'

I could happily pick up any one of these and start to write a story. They all do something that's vital in fiction; they make the reader ask questions.

Where is Annie and what's the significance of the cars?

Can the person really read Steven like a book, or can Steven read them?

What happened at the vet?

What's the significance of the pavolva and why did they choose to make one yesterday? How did it turn out? Had they made it before? Were they trying to impress somebody? What happened?

Finally we have Sandra Roberts. It's unlikely that she really is invisible. It's far more likely that she just feels that way because people aren't taking any notice of her, but what if she really WAS invisible? How did that happen?

When you've played with a set of opening lines, it's time to read the actual stories.

You will probably find that your story outlines don't resemble the finished product at all. This is why you can go to any creative writing class and give people exactly the same prompt, and everyone will produce something different. Don't be shy. Go ahead. Borrow a few first lines and titles. If you're at all worried, you can always change them round a bit.

For example, here's an opening line from one of my short stories.

'As Trish stepped into Ken's garden, she felt her heart sink.'

If the story wasn't mine and I wanted to borrow this opening line, I could alter it like this.

'The moment Ann stepped into her neighbour's garden, her heart sank.'

The words are different, but the sense has stayed the same. More importantly, the same questions are raised in the reader's mind – why does her heart sink?

Exercise

Beg, borrow or buy a copy of *Woman's Weekly Fiction Special*.

Note down some of the opening lines to the stories and see where they take you.

Don't forget that you can also find first lines in books, plays, films and newspaper articles.

Fortune Telling and The Occult

Many people are fascinated by the occult. This explains the popularity of magazines with titles such as *Chat It's Fate* and *Take a Break's Fate and Fortune*. It also explains why stories with a fortune telling theme are actively sought after by fiction editors.

There are many ways of seeing into the future – crystal balls, runes, palm reading, tea leaves, tarot cards and so on. Choose one you are familiar with or know something about, then start asking those questions.

Firstly, who is the story about? Is it the fortune teller or the person having their fortune read?

What is the prediction? Does it come true? Is the fortune teller real or a fake?

Try out your cast of characters and see how they react when somebody offers to tell them the future.

Of course, the fortune teller might not even be human.

This story was published in *My Weekly*.

MR MAGICA TELLS YOUR FORTUNE.

Paul stared at the old machine. He knew Paignton Pier like the back of his hand. The Psychic Sarah machine should be standing in this spot, not something called Mr Magica.

Coloured lights twinkled, holding his gaze. A disembodied head, topped with a garish orange and purple turban, sat inside the glass case. It looked as if it belonged in a house of horrors, not part of a fortune telling machine.

Paul found himself unable to resist the pull of the staring eyes, and stepped closer. Before he knew what he was doing, he'd pushed a £1 coin into the slot. As he placed his hands, palms down on the pad, the machine whirred and rumbled until a poorly printed card dropped into the tray with a clunk.

'Speak to a stranger and your broken heart will mend.'

A cold shiver ran down Paul's neck. The machine couldn't know about his break-up with Claire. It was just a silly coincidence.

Just then, he noticed a young woman sitting on a bench, gazing into the middle distance. Thinking about Mr Magica's prediction, he walked over to her before he could lose his nerve.

"Mind if I join you?" he asked.

"Yes," she said as she stood up and walked off.

He was about to throw the card away, but something stopped him. After all, it didn't say the first stranger, did it? He soon saw another young woman, leaning on the rails and gazing out to sea.

"Lovely day, isn't it?" he said.

"Yes. The sky's so blue. It's like being on the Med."

He stood next to her. "I've been coming here on holiday for as long as I can remember. My grandparents...."

A hand pushed his arm roughly before he had a chance to say anything else. "Oi! Push off, that's my girlfriend you're chatting up."

A giant of a man stood over him, brandishing two ice creams like clubs. "Sorry," Paul said, as he walked briskly away.

He wandered away from the pier. Just how many strangers did he have to talk to before he could give up and go back to his hotel room? And why was he even bothering to do what Mr Magica had told him to do? It was just a stupid machine after all.

Coming back to Paignton already felt like a big mistake. The scattering of shells, the rich brown sand, even the stalls selling ice cream and candy floss; everything reminded him of happier times, times he'd spent with Claire. It wasn't a good place to be alone with an aching heart. His head bowed, he walked down the steps on to the beach. Without thinking, he kicked a pebble.

"Watch what you're doing!" shouted an angry voice.

"Sorry!" said Paul.

He stared out to sea, watching the waves. What he did, was up to him. He could wallow in self pity or he could keep trying, and do what the machine had suggested. He decided to have one more try and speak to the next person he saw. This turned out to be two ladies, visiting Torbay for the first time.

"Lovely day, isn't it?" he said.

"Yes. Every time we come to Devon, the sun shines," one of the ladies replied.

"Have you been here before?" the other lady asked.

"Many times," he said.

"Good, then maybe you could suggest somewhere to eat."

Paul was pleased to help. The ladies were both older than his mother, but that didn't matter, at least they'd been happy to talk to him. That made him feel so much better.

He decided to give it an hour. During that time, he'd talk to as many strangers as he could. The reactions he got were mixed; everything from rudeness and sarcasm, to caution and polite lack of interest.

He checked his watch before walking over to an attractive brunette. There was still plenty of time. "Hello," he said. "My name's Paul."

Her eyes lit up as she grabbed hold of his arm. "Tina! Pam! Donna! I've got one."

At once he was surrounded by a giggling group of women.

One of them squeezed his biceps. "Bit scrawny," she said and they all laughed. It didn't take long for the penny to drop. He'd stumbled into a hen party.

"Fancy doing a striptease for us?" one of them said with a grin.

"Sorry. I have to be somewhere," he said, but the ladies blocked his way.

"Not so fast," said one woman. "We could use some male company, couldn't we girls?"

He let himself be dragged back onto the pier, joining in as the girlfriends bowled balls, shot at targets, and fished for fluffy bears. At last they tired of their new toy, and let him get away.

"Oh well," he thought, as he checked the time, "that was fun, and at least I TRIED talking to people."

As he headed back through the jumble of amusement machines, he spotted a young woman standing next to the Mr Magica machine. "Don't waste your money," he called out. "It's useless."

The girl stopped, coin poised in the air. *"Why do you say that?"*

He showed her his card. *"I did what it told me to do. As a result, I've been chased, shouted at and threatened. I nearly had my clothes ripped off too,"* he said, as he explained about the hen night.

"Oh dear." The girl laughed as she dropped the coin back into her purse. *"Been here long?"* she asked him.

"No, I only arrived this morning but I'm beginning to think it was a mistake," and he told her about Claire and their break-up and how he'd needed to get away.

"I know what will make you feel better," she said. *"A great big ice cream with a flake. It always works for me."*

"You're on," he said. *"I'm Paul."*

"Meg," she replied. *"Pleased to meet you."*

Later as they sat on the sea wall eating their ice creams, she asked if he felt any better.

"Much," he said.

"Then I'd better be off. I'm meeting my folks for dinner."

"Do you have to go?" he asked.

She nodded. *"But we could meet up later if you like."*

They spent the next three days together.

On her last evening, Paul took Meg's hand in his. *"We don't live very far from each other. I'd like to see you again, after we get home."*

"Best not," she told him. *"This is just a holiday romance. They never last, do they?"*

He wrote down his mobile number and gave it to her. *"If you change your mind, give me a call,"* then he kissed her goodbye.

The next morning, Meg went for a last look round the town. Without knowing why, she wandered on to the pier and soon found herself standing next to Mr Magica. The machine's deep metallic voice whispered to her. *"I can tell you the future,"* it said.

After making sure nobody was watching, she pulled out a coin and fed it into the machine, then placed her palm on the pad.

A printed card popped out into the tray. *'Your true love waits. All you have to do is call.'*

She laughed. "OK, OK, I give in," she said and then she tapped out Paul's number on her mobile.

It was a much happier Paul who came back to Paignton six months later. He and Meg had just got engaged. They strolled on to the pier, arm in arm, wanting to thank the machine that had brought them together, but Mr Magica wasn't there. Psychic Sara was there instead, where she'd always been.

It was as if Mr Magica had never even existed.

The idea for that story came to me when I lived in Paignton in Devon. One day I was on the pier, wasting a few pennies in various machines when I spotted this fortune telling machine.

I couldn't resist trying it out. I can't recall what the printed card said, but whatever it was started me thinking – how could somebody try to make a prediction come true?

I imagined a man who'd recently broken up with his girlfriend, and the story grew from there.

As well as all the different ways fortunes can be told, there are other aspects of the occult, such as spells and magic.

In *Aladdin*, there's a magic lamp that when rubbed produces a genie who is able to grant wishes. What other kinds of everyday objects could be magical in some way? What if somebody found an old book of spells? Would the story end well or badly? What would YOU do if you found a magic lamp? What would be your three wishes? How would you cope with that sudden feeling of power?

The beauty of the short story is that you don't need to go into lengthy explanations. If you want to introduce a magic computer, you can.

The only limits are your own imagination.

Ghosts and Spirits

I don't write very many ghost stories. The best ones rely heavily on atmosphere, while I prefer to deal with characters and relationships, but if ghostly happenings appeal to you, there are lots of ways to generate those spooky ideas.

A good place to start is in your hometown. A quick internet search will reveal any nearby haunted pubs or houses and will give you enough background for a short story. You might even be able to visit the location to soak up the atmosphere.

Ghost stories often have a twist (think of the well known film starring Bruce Willis, *The Sixth Sense*). Quite often the narrator of the story turns out to be the ghost. Finding an original slant on this twist might prove difficult.

If I wanted to write an original ghost story, I would probably do this. I would choose a different genre, like romance, cowboys and Indians, science fiction or horror, and add a ghost to the mix. Ghostly animals are worth a thought too.

Séances, where a group of people try to make contact with 'the other side' via a medium, are also popular.

Again, all you need to do is ask questions.

Is the medium real or fake? If they are fake, what do they hope to gain?

What is their motive? Are they trying to contact somebody themselves? If so, why is that the one voice that never comes through?

Why are the people attending the séance there?

What do they want to hear?

What happens when a voice does come through? Does it say something unexpected or something that somebody listening finds too true for comfort?

In the hugely popular film *Ghost*, Whoopi Goldberg stars as a fake medium, shocked to find that she really can contact the dead. This is another basic idea that can easily be stolen or adapted.

As you can see, séances make great starting points for stories. It helps that they normally take place in dark, enclosed rooms where the atmosphere is already claustrophobic. Thanks to television programmes, books and films, most people know what happens at a séance, even if they have never been to one.

As regards to a more straightforward ghost story, it might be worth giving some thought to what it is that is actually haunted. It doesn't need to be a building like a house or a castle; objects can be haunted too.

For example, what might happen if a man's computer or sat nav became possessed by the spirit of his dead wife? How might a mobile phone, haunted by its murdered owner, bring the killer to justice?

As you can see, a ghost story can be more than just a ghost story. It can cover crime, romance, even science fiction. All you have to do is ask those questions and open your mind.

Halloween

October 31st, otherwise known as All Hallows Eve, has grown increasingly important as a holiday, thanks to the American custom of trick or treat, which has started to become popular in this country. That means that magazine editors will probably want to mark the occasion by using at least one Halloween story.

One of the simplest ways to come up with an idea for Halloween is to do some research. Look up customs and traditions associated with October 31st on the internet and you will find all kinds of superstitions attached to that date, any of which can lead you into a story.

You will find that searching for true love features in many of these ancient customs and traditions. Again, a quick internet search will result in dozens to choose from.

One of the most well known goes like this. If you peel an apple in one piece, the shape it forms will be the initial letter of your future love's name and before you ask, no, I haven't tried it, yet.

There are also spells that you can cast on Halloween in order to find love. I found one that required burning an orange candle. This one, I have done. Whether it works, only time will tell.

Trick or treating is also fertile ground for ideas to grow in. Try out the characters from your cast list and see how they react when a succession of children knock on their door, demanding treats.

You might also consider an updated or reworked fairy tale as several of those feature witches, good or bad.

For example, you might want to feature the fairy godmother from *Cinderella* and show how she indulges her wicked side at Halloween. What if all the good fairies get together once a year for a night of trick or treating?

Exercise

Find a tradition or superstition relating to Halloween.

Now think about a character who might want to follow one and ask yourself why this is, and what could possibly go wrong with their plans.

Finally, figure out what happens in the end and tie that up with their original intention – has it finished badly, or worked out well in the end?

Congratulations, you have just come up with another plot for a story.

Headlines

Headlines are great starting points for stories as they are designed to grab the attention, as well as giving a strong hint as to what the article that follows is about.

I find that the most useful ones can be found in local papers.

Here are a few examples taken from a copy of *The Weekly News*. (If you haven't heard of this paper, it comes from DC Thomson and is more like a magazine than a newspaper. It also carries two short stories each week so is a good market as well as a source of ideas. It's normally hidden on the bottom shelf next to *The Angling Times*.)

'Edith terrified by Mum's message.'

What was the message? Maybe her Mum is dead, so how could she be calling? (ghost story)

'Donating blood led to romance.'

A romance in a blood donor van, now that could be different.

'Dig yourself out of depression.'

Who could be digging? Where? Does it work? Who do they meet?

'Crooks target designer dogs.'

If you want an unusual crime story, this sounds as though it could be a good place to start.

'Holiday regret for old ravers.'

This one really grabbed my attention. It was followed by a very short article telling how many people in their thirties regret not having gone on an 18-30 holiday (holidays designed for young people with a reputation for being rather wild) when they had the chance.

That made me wonder about somebody much older, and what regrets they might have. I don't know about you, but I certainly wish I'd given one of those holidays a try when I was younger.

The fact is, every one of these headlines represents a potential starting point, and they all came from just one edition of one paper.

All kinds of stories are covered in local newspapers. Everything from feel-good pieces about lost dogs being found after five years, to graphic accounts of serious crimes.

As you read that headline, why not imagine you were one of the people involved and tell their story?

Next time you sit down to read the Sunday papers, make sure you have that notepad close to hand.

Hobbies

Most of us have hobbies of one kind or another, so you might want to start this section by making a list of your hobbies and interests.

To leave the subject of fiction for a moment, if you are especially good at any of them, this could be the time to think about writing articles for specialist magazines.

When we are good at something we often don't realise that other people find what we take for granted much more difficult. For example, I find it incredibly easy to come up with ideas. I always thought that other writers would find it just as simple. If I had realised that wasn't the case, I would have written this book years ago.

If you subscribe to, or buy, any specialist magazines, next time you read one, check to see if there are openings for any articles. If there are, write a paragraph outlining your idea and send it to the editor.

Now to return to fiction. If you enjoy one of the more popular hobbies such as cooking or gardening, you will already have enough information to provide a backdrop to a story.

The even better news is that the many fiction readers who share your interest will, as soon as they see what your story is about, want to read it. For example, a quick glance at the fiction in an issue of *The People's Friend* usually reveals at least one story with either a gardening or a cookery theme.

Once you have your chosen subject, it's time to think about problems and conflict. What kind of problem could somebody who likes to knit face? (Replace the word knit with the hobby or interest you are familiar with) A knitter might face a shortage of funds to buy wool, lack of time to pursue their hobby, maybe even rivalry with another knitter in a forthcoming race or sponsored event.

How do they solve the problem? If they are short of materials, they could ask for donations of wool and end up with far more than they could handle. What do they do then?

When you ask questions like this, it's important to write down ALL the answers that come to you, however daft they may sound. These daft ideas can, with a little bit more thought, lead to the best stories.

Maybe you don't have any hobbies. In that case, are there any games you like to play? I'm thinking of board games like Scrabble and Monopoly, or card games like Cribbage and Bridge. Again, any of these can make an intriguing backdrop to fiction.

I used to play Bridge and loved every minute, but there were often times when I could cheerfully have murdered my partner, and times when they probably felt the same way about me. There's definitely a crime story in there somewhere.

These days, computer and console games are almost as good as the real thing. This makes them suitable hunting grounds for stories with twist endings.

For example, the story appears to be about a game of tennis when the characters are actually playing tennis on a Nintendo Wii games console. I once wrote a story where it looked as though the people were enjoying a round of golf but they were actually playing crazy golf at the seaside.

Another example of one of my stories follows to show you how this idea might work in practice.

Now that you have been forewarned and are looking for the twist, you should be able to spot it very early on. All the same, try and look for the clues that were put there to mislead a more innocent reader.

The story stars my very own amateur sleuth, Dorothy Peters, who featured in a series of stories published in *My Weekly*. Her adventures can also be found in my first collection of stories, *Crime*, available on Kindle.

WATCHING THE DETECTIVES

Sergeant Cooper introduced Dorothy to his colleagues. "That's Detective Inspector Grainger sitting by the window, and opposite him is Detective Constable Palmer."

Dorothy stood, hesitating, in the doorway. "I'm not sure this is such a good idea," she whispered.

"Nonsense," the Sergeant said as he strode to the other side of the room. "They've been dying to meet you ever since I mentioned your crime solving skills. Now, come on in and don't be shy."

Dorothy began to wish she hadn't told him about her recent adventures.

It had all started when Howard Keen's prize winning koi started to disappear from his pond. The fish were worth hundreds of pounds. He suspected a gang of thieves, eager to make a quick profit, but Dorothy had other ideas.

Once she'd spotted the footprints in the mud, it was easy to work out that the culprit wasn't actually human; it was Joan Wood's newly adopted cat. A hastily erected net soon put an end to the cat's fishing expeditions. Howard told everyone how Dorothy had "solved the crime". Ever since then, all kinds of people had asked for her help.

So far, she'd managed to outwit a dodgy roofer, and worked out that a mysterious intruder was actually the householder's estranged wife. In that case she'd not only solved the crime, she'd mended a marriage at the same time. But none of those crimes had been serious, and they were all easy to solve. All she'd had to do was use her commonsense, and spot some fairly obvious clues.

Murder was in a very different league.

Nobody had ever asked her to help solve one of those before and it wasn't a straightforward killing either. There were six possible culprits, each of whom had a strong motive.

Reluctantly, she put on a smile and followed Sergeant Cooper into the room and took her seat. It was too late to back out now. All she could do was try her best.

As she glanced across at the Sergeant, her heart skipped. They'd been dating for three months now, and she still found it hard to concentrate when he was close by. She'd retired to the sleepy Devon village five years after losing her husband, intending to live out her remaining years, peacefully and quietly. Instead, she'd fallen head over heels in love. The strength of her feelings constantly surprised her - she was sixty-one, not sixteen.

As if reading her mind, the Sergeant mouthed the words, "Are you OK?"

She nodded and with a struggle turned her thoughts back to the crime. Unless she concentrated, she could end up making a fool of herself.

As the details began to emerge, Dorothy fought to control her nerves. She still had no idea who had committed the crime but from what the others were saying, it was obvious that nobody else in the room did either. All she had to do was stay calm and try to think straight. Unfortunately, that was proving more difficult than she'd hoped.

Being in the same room with three police officers was doing nothing to steady her nerves. Even though she'd never done anything even remotely dishonest in her entire life, she couldn't help feeling anxious. The atmosphere was heavy with tension, and full of expectation. She knew that everyone was waiting to hear what she, a mere civilian, had to say, wondering if she would be able to solve the crime.

It was her own fault. She should never have told the Sergeant about her skill as a detective. She should have realised he'd want to put them to the test.

She took a deep breath and tried to concentrate on the facts. Gradually, she started to put the evidence together, piece by piece, until at last the full picture began to emerge.

"I think I know who did it," she said, trying to sound more confident than she felt.

Sergeant Cooper turned towards her, the hint of a smile playing on his lips. "Really? Well that's amazing. I still don't have a clue."

"Nor me," agreed the Detective Inspector. "So who was it?"

The room fell silent as Dorothy took a deep breath then made her accusation in a clear voice. "Am I right?" she asked nervously.

The Inspector picked up the cards and frowned. "Yes. Miss Scarlet in the library with the candlestick. Remind me never to play Cluedo with you again."

Out of sight of the others, Sergeant Cooper gave Dorothy a wink.

She smiled. It seemed she'd passed his test with flying colours.

You may have found it easy to guess that they were playing a game because I'd already told you that before you started to read, but would you have guessed the twist so easily otherwise? Hopefully not. This kind of twist has lots of potential and can work well. The important thing to do is make sure that the reader understands the denouement. In other words, stories where the characters turn out to be playing Monopoly or Scrabble are fine as most readers will have played, or at least heard of, those games, but if you based a story on the card game Cribbage, or the board game Risk, many readers will feel cheated. They need to be able to look back and say, yes, of course, why didn't I figure that out sooner?

It's all about remembering to keep your average reader in mind.

You may know the rules of Chess and understand the Sicilian defence, but if your reader has never played the game, they won't be able to fully enjoy the story.

Hobbies are also a good way to throw people off the gender scent. In other words, if a character enjoys knitting, the reader is likely to assume they are female (see *Twist Endings*).

Holidays, Summer

There is a good market for holiday and summer stories. According to magazine editors at least, the holiday season lasts for several months (I wish it did where I live!), which means the demand for stories with a summery theme is higher than for any other kind of fiction.

Due to timescales, I generally start to think about writing holiday stories in January.

The bad news is that it can be difficult to think of sunshine and lovely warm weather when you have just shovelled up six inches of snow from the driveway. The good news is that it's immediately after Christmas that newspapers start filling their pages with holidays ads.

As with any other seasonal kind of story, I keep a special file in which anything that might help me to come up with an idea gets filed away.

These might be articles on different kinds of holidays, readers' letters telling of holidays that went well or very badly, short stories from last summer that I enjoyed reading, pictures from magazines, postcards and so on.

Make notes of as many of your own holidays as you can think of.

Don't forget to include day trips and the times you stayed with relatives. If your memory is as sieve-like as mine is, you might want to do this as and when you think of something, and jot it down in a special notebook.

For each holiday or trip, make some brief notes of the things you most remember about it, good or bad as well as those all important telling details. Here are a few prompts to get the memory cells sparking.

Have you had any holiday romances? If so, how did they turn out?

Have you ever been disappointed when you arrived at a hotel, resort or camp site? Did you make the most of it or not?

Were you, or anyone you travelled with, taken ill or injured while they were away?

Did you ever make your holiday sound much better than it was?

When thinking about summer holidays, it's easy just to think of clear skies, blue seas and perfect weather, but we all know that the truth is often very far removed from that ideal.

Often when we look back, we remember the good times, and forget about most of the bad bits.

The following story grew directly from that idea.

It was published in *My Weekly*.

AN ENGLISH SUMMER

"You stay here. There's no point in us both getting wet."

As I watch Alex leave the café, I let out a sigh. It's all going so horribly wrong. Alex is only here for another four days. I need his trip to be perfect. Need him to fall back in love with Devon.

So far we've been to Killerton House and got caught in a storm at the farthest end of the gardens, with only trees for cover. Then we visited a village fete where the wind came up so strong it blew books off tables as easy as seeds off a dandelion clock and whipped my hair into torturous knots. The next day, we took a trip to London to visit Wimbledon, but the train was delayed for two hours. When we finally arrived, did we see any tennis? Not a stroke. Just rain, and more rain.

Now I'm sitting here, in a lovely café in Sidmouth, struggling to make out anything through the rain streaked glass. Waiting for Alex to return with the car.

Throughout June, it's been warm and sunny, every single day, but as soon as Alex arrived, the weather changed. A cold front from the North Atlantic, at least that's what Sian the weather girl said. I look out into the pelting rain, then peer into the distance searching for a hint of blue. Nothing. Grey, grey, grey.

Alex was my first sweetheart. We grew up together. There was never anyone else for me. When he was offered a post in an Australian hospital, I was devastated. He asked me to marry him, but I didn't have the courage to tear up my English roots.

We kept in touch for a year, but gradually our calls and letters got further apart until one day they stopped. Some time later, I heard he'd married an Australian girl. I wished him good luck and got on with my life. Of course, I dated, even got engaged once, but I couldn't go through with it. No one could replace Alex.

I came across him thirty years later, completely by accident. I was online, ordering the latest Minette Walters novel, when his name came into my head. On a whim, I typed it into the computer, never expecting to find anything. Up popped 2256 references and 186 web pages. I had no idea there'd be so many people out there called Alex Graham. Without much hope, I checked a few sites, only to find myself suddenly looking at a photo of my Alex.

In no time, I was reading all about him and looking at photos of him and his family. I read every word, every link. I discovered he was about to retire from the private practice he ran with his two sons, and that his wife had died suddenly in 1994, the same year my mother died.

On impulse I sent an e-mail, regretting my hasty act as soon as my finger left the send button. For five days I didn't dare turn on the computer. I don't know why. Was I afraid he'd reply or terrified he wouldn't? Would he have forgotten all about me?

I keep that first e-mail he sent, safe in my box of treasures.

It reads, 'Lovely to hear from you after so many years. How's dear old England?'

We were soon e-mailing each other every day. Then two months ago, he sent the words I'd been dreading, yet longing for. 'Missing the English summer so much I'm coming over on a visit. Arrive June 28*th*. Have you got a spare room? '

So here I am on a cold, wet, windy day. The third of July but you wouldn't know it.

I look up to see Alex has returned. My car's parked right outside the door.

"I'm so sorry Alex. Everything's going wrong." I begin to cry." You must be wishing you hadn't bothered."

I dab at my tears with a Kleenex. He looks at me. I know he's trying to look severe, but he can't keep it up.

"How can you grin like that when I'm so upset?" I blubber.

"I can't help it, Susan. You look like a two year old who's dropped her ice cream."

"I do not," I say.

He nods and smiles at me.

I wipe my tears away and pout. "Well maybe I do, but I wanted this holiday to be perfect. When you said how much you missed England in the summertime..."

He helps me on with my coat, then reaches over and puts a finger on my lips. "This IS summer, Susan. This is how I remember dear old Blighty - not sunshine. Not blue skies. When I think of England I think of us, sheltering under umbrellas that were too small, stepping into puddles, getting drenched when buses went by. "

"Like that day in Bristol," I say my tears gone.

"You got soaked the minute we got off the train."

"I squelched all day"

"But you didn't mind," he says.

"No, I didn't mind. I was young and in love."

"I know," says Alex. His grey eyes grow serious. "It's not the sunshine or the scenery I remember from that last summer, it's you, Susan. YOU are an English summer to me."

He cups my face in his hands and draws me gently towards him. As we share our first kiss in thirty years, I know summer has truly arrived at last. We step out into the rain together.

I have written several stories on the theme of rain spoiling holiday plans and how memory can be selective, as both of these scenarios are things that most people can relate to.

Since the economy went into recession, another theme I keep returning to is affordability. For example, what people might do if they can't afford to go to Spain for their holiday?

They could go somewhere else and find it's just as expensive. They could stay home and lie about where they've been. If they do that, what happens? Are they found out?

Again, going away on holiday with somebody else can be fertile ground for ideas. What if you discover that you don't get on quite as well with your best friend as you thought you did or that your friend/sister/brother expects you to act as chief, free, babysitter to their dreadful/adorable children? What if you found yourself trapped in a small caravan with your nearest and dearest while the rain lashed down outside? How long would it be before something snapped?

There is so much potential for conflict here, and we haven't even looked at the weather, problems understanding the language, unusual food and so on.

Hopefully you can see that coming up with ideas for holiday stories is not as hard as you thought it was.

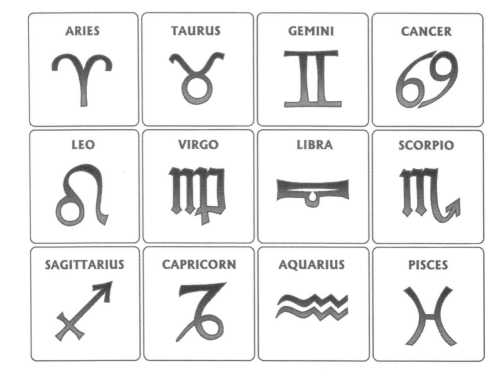

Horoscopes

Like millions of people, I find horoscopes fascinating.

My birthday is on 28th June, which makes me a Cancerian.

I'm supposed to get on with other water signs (Scorpio and Pisces), as well as my opposite sign of Capricorn and find that, in general, that is the case. I also have problems with Geminis (and Aquarian males but it's probably best not to go into that here).

Whether you believe in the stars or not doesn't matter, because you can still use horoscopes to generate ideas for fiction.

Imagine one of your stock characters sitting down to read their horoscope. How does it come true (or not)?

Here's an example for Sagittarius. 'Be careful that you don't promise more than you can deliver.'

What might happen if your character read that forecast when they've just come off the phone having volunteered to run the book stall at the church's Christmas Fair? Or you might choose an absent father who has just told his son that he will buy the games console he wants, even though he knows he can't afford it.

It's all about imagining what the horoscope could mean to a person and whether or not they choose to believe it. Just read through a set of predictions and see if any of them appeal to you.

An idea that comes up quite frequently, but is still worth considering, goes like this – somebody reads their horoscope not believing a word of it, but as the day goes on, each little bit of it comes true.

What happens at the end is up to you.

Here's another one to think about. What if the heroine will only date Leos? How does a man born under another sign get round this?

I also like to use astrology to help me come up with three dimensional characters.

I have several books on the subject, my favourite being Linda Goodman's *Sun Signs*. Inside there are sixty well rounded character types, five for each star sign – man, woman, child, boss and employee. You get the whole personality, good points and bad, so that you can't help but create a believable character.

Chinese Astrology can be fertile ground too. There you have twelve different animal signs according to the year a person is born in. I'm a sheep, sometimes called a goat.

Again, any book on the subject will give you the good and bad side of each of the signs, which I find incredibly useful.

This is what Chinese astrology has to say about me. Sensitive, and very creative, goats are honest, sincere people who look for the best in others. All good so far, but then there are the not so nice goat qualities – anxious and disorganised, gullible, careless and so on.

I'd like to say that I have all the goat's positive qualities and none of the bad, but I can't, I'm too honest.

Joking aside, the potted character sketches these books provide are invaluable. They make lovely ready-made stock characters if you don't want to go to the trouble of inventing your own.

Illnesses and Allergies

We've all been ill at some time so why not use that experience as the basis of a story? Your first hand knowledge will add that much needed ring of truth.

What effect did the illness have in the long or short term? Did it change any relationships? Did you get as many cards or visitors as expected? If not, why?

It's often the case that we don't find out who our real friends are until we need them. What would happen if a character pretended to be ill or injured? Why would they want to do this?

Even minor illnesses can be good starting points.

I used to suffer from hay fever very badly indeed when I was younger so I know what it feels like and what a nuisance it can be.

Other people could enjoy their gardens, but one sniff of a rose, and I was in trouble. I used to dread examinations as they always took place right when the pollen count was at its highest. I have no idea how I managed to pass any of them.

For me, having hay fever was a major inconvenience, but I learned to live with it, but what if a sufferer was invited to a garden party at Buckingham Palace one summer?

The following story occurred to me when a friend of mine announced they were planning a June wedding.

It was published in *Take A Break's Fiction Feast*.

JUNE WEDDING

"You're getting married!" Lynne hugged her sister. "That's great news. Have you set a date yet?"

"Yes. June 28th," replied Anna.

"Oh dear," said Lynne.

"What's wrong? I thought you were happy for me."

"I am, but June. That's right in the middle of the hay fever season. My nose will be bright red."

"I'd forgotten about that," replied Anna. "Does it matter?"

"Not if you don't mind me ruining the wedding photos with my Rudolph the red nosed reindeer impression."

Anna laughed. "I'm sorry, sis, but there's nothing I can do. It's the only time David can get time off."

"Don't worry," said Lynne. "Maybe my doctor can help."

She went to see him after work the next day. "My sister's getting married in June. I get such terrible hay fever. Is there anything you can do?"

The doctor flicked through her notes. "You've already tried most things. You've got a nose spray and eye drops. Frankly, there's not much else I can do. It will get better as you get older," he said cheerfully.

"I need it to get better now," she said.

"I could give you stronger tablets but they'll make you feel sleepy, plus you wouldn't be able to drink alcohol while you're taking them. Do you want to try those?"

"I'm not sure. I don't fancy falling asleep at my sister's wedding."

The doctor smiled. "I'll write a prescription then you can decide whether you want to use it."

She thought about it on her way home. This was her sister's wedding. She didn't want to drop off and miss most of it. Worse still, if she couldn't drink, she couldn't join in the toast. She threw the prescription away. It would be better to suffer. There weren't likely to be any single men at the wedding and if the pollen count stayed low, she wouldn't have a problem.

The day of the wedding soon arrived. Lynne looked out of the window. It was dry but overcast. If it didn't get hot or breezy, she'd be fine.

The car picked her up at eleven. Her sister was already at the registry office.

"You look beautiful, Anna," Lynne told her.

"You don't look too bad yourself. How's your nose holding up?"

Lynne laughed. "Fine, so far."

Just then, the groom appeared and they went inside.

As the room filled up with friends and family, Lynne relaxed. There wasn't an eligible bachelor in sight. It wouldn't matter if her nose did turn red.

Then a man walked through the door. Tall, slim, casually dressed but with a presence she could almost feel. She looked for an accompanying female but there wasn't one.

He took a seat on the other side of the room. During the ceremony, she glanced across, only to find that he was looking back at her.

She prayed the weather would stay dull, but the moment the ceremony was over, and they went outside for the photos, a breeze began to rustle the leaves. The sun was high in a clear blue cloudless sky and the temperature was climbing steadily. It was a perfect day for a wedding. It was also a perfect day for hay fever. Lynne could almost feel the pollen count creeping up.

She sighed and let herself be ordered about by the photographer. Suddenly she found herself standing next to the mystery man.

"Hi. My name's Nick. I'm David's cousin." He held out his hand and as their fingers touched, Lynne shivered as a tingle went down her arm

"Pleased to meet you. I'm Lynne. The bride's sister,"

"Are you here on your own?" he whispered.

"Yes."

"Didn't the boyfriend want to come?"

"I'm single," she said.

"Good," he grinned.

Lynne swallowed hard. Trust her to meet a man, today of all days.

"Rob didn't tell me you were gorgeous. If he had, I'd have come down before."

Lynne blushed, suddenly tongue-tied.

"Do you fancy going out sometime?" he asked her.

"Maybe," she said.

Just then the photographer barked out another instruction. "Bride's family now please."

129

"I've got to go," Nick said. "I'll catch you later."

Lynne's nose started to itch the moment they got back to her mother's house for the reception. She got through the speeches with a few sniffs and a couple of sneezes, but her symptoms were getting steadily worse.

She went to the bathroom to survey the damage. Her eyes were puffy and starting to itch. She needed her eye drops badly. With a sigh, she removed her mascara and eye shadow. Once the drops were in, her eyes felt less prickly, even if they were rather red.

"What a mess," she said to her reflection. "When Nick sees me like this, that'll be that."

She sighed dismally, used her nose spray, and went back to join the party.

The first person she bumped into was Nick. "Good gracious. What's happened to you?" he said. "You look terrible."

She ran from the room, and headed back upstairs to the safety of her old room. If Nick was the kind of man who only cared what she looked like, then he was no loss. She pulled herself together. This was her sister's wedding. It wasn't the time to get upset.

When she went back downstairs, Nick was nowhere to be seen.

"Congratulations, Mrs Cameron," she gave her sister a big hug. "You too, brother-in-law."

David grinned. "Thanks, Lynne. What happened to your face?"

Anna elbowed her bridegroom in the ribs. "Ignore him. You look fine."

Lynne laughed. "No, I don't. Anyway, have a great honeymoon. I'll see you both when you get back."

She went to the back door to get some air. There, she spotted Nick. He was sitting on a bench in the garden, his head bowed.

Her first thought was to ignore him. He'd been rude to her, why should she care about him? Besides, the garden was full of roses. If that didn't set her off on a sneezing marathon, nothing would, but she couldn't just leave him there, sitting by himself, not when he looked so upset.

She sighed wearily and went over. "Hi, it's me, Lynne."

He nodded, but he didn't look up.

"Mind if I sit down for a moment?" she said.

"Help yourself," he said.

She sat down, feeling rather uncomfortable. "Anna and David make a lovely couple, don't you think?"

"Yes."

It was no use. She couldn't make him talk, if he didn't want to. She got up to leave. "Bye then," she said.

"Wait. Don't go. When I said you looked terrible, I didn't mean anything, I just meant........." As he spoke, he lifted his head.

Lynne gasped. His eyes were red and swollen. "What's wrong? Have you had some bad news?"

"I'm fine, but I'm horribly allergic to cats. Five minutes with your mum's Siamese and I was gone."

Lynne laughed.

"What's funny?" he asked her. "I look a mess."

"So do I" she pulled a bottle of eye drops from her bag. "Try this." She handed the bottle to him. "I always carry a spare."

Just then the breeze strengthened, blowing the scent of roses their way. Lynne sneezed. It was a while before she could say anything else. When she could speak, she pointed to the flower bed. "I've got terrible hay fever. Those roses are setting me off." She blew her nose loudly. "The doctor gave me a prescription, but if I'd taken the tablets, I'd probably have nodded off."

"When I saw you earlier, with your pink eyes, I didn't mean to sound rude. It was just a shock to see a fellow sufferer." He smiled and took her free hand. "So the red eyed look doesn't put you off?" he asked.

"No. Besides, if we stay out here, my eyes will soon be as red as yours."

She sneezed again, and he laughed. "Would your hay fever be better down by the river?"

She nodded and sneezed at the same time.

"Apparently there's a cosy pub down there. Definitely no cats. What do you say? Shall we take a wander?"

"Atishoo," was her only reply.

Hopefully that story will help you to see the potential for stories featuring allergies. Other minor ailments can also cause major problems. Think for a moment about laryngitis.

That's not too much of a handicap on a day to day basis, but if a man loses his voice the day before he's due to give a speech at his daughter's wedding, or has an interview for a new job, the consequences can be massive.

Exercise

Write a list of as many minor aliments as you can think of. What problems could each of these cause?

Major illnesses and disabilities can also be used as starting points for ideas.

I remember a story where a woman liked a man but he was in a wheelchair so she didn't ask him out. It turned out that he wasn't disabled at all; he was simply trying out the chair to see for himself the problems that wheelchair users faced.

I've also read stories where the main character turns out to be blind or deaf.

Personally, I prefer to leave this kind of story to other writers. You could call it one of my hang-ups.

I also avoid stories about people who are seriously ill. This may be due to the fact that I've been lucky as regards to physical ailments. I haven't suffered from anything more serious than asthma and tonsillitis. I also find such stories hard to take. I usually end up feeling as though my emotions have been manipulated in some way.

We all have subjects we enjoy writing about, and those we would rather avoid. This is one of mine. That said, if you feel happy about writing about these subjects and can handle them with sensitivity, then go ahead. Due to their high emotional content, they often find a market.

Jokes

Sadly, most jokes don't translate into good stories. They might appear to, but they're usually far too two dimensional and often rely on a surprise ending.

Isaac Asimov sometimes wrote stories where the last line was actually a punchline, or some other kind of play on words, but this technique has fallen out of favour, although you might find a home for it on the internet.

I prefer to look at cartoons for inspiration – not the serious ones with a political message, but the light-hearted variety such as those drawn by Matt in *The Telegraph*.

Many of the best cartoons are about relationships between two or more people and say so much with a few, very well chosen words.

Next time you see a cartoon, don't just laugh at it, think about it. Is there a story in there?

The following examples come from one issue of *The Weekly News*.

One cartoon showed two men, drinking beer, up to their waists in foam. One says to the other, "Good head on this home brew."

I imagined a house where every cupboard was crammed with demijohns and containers, each one full of fermenting wine or beer. What would the brewer's spouse have to say about that? And what, if anything, would she do to try and change it?

Another showed a man bent over at an angle of ninety degrees with his doctor asking how his cycling holiday went.

That gave me an idea about a woman who went cycling to impress a man, but ended up aching and covered in bruises instead. I went on to sell that story to a magazine in Australia.

Another cartoon showed a woman in a library looking at a medical book. Fixed to the end of the shelf is a bottle of smelling salts ready to revive anyone who faints after reading it.

That set me off wondering about somebody who each time they heard of a new disease imagined they were suffering from it – in other words, a typical hypochondriac. How would their partner cope? What would happen if they were ever, genuinely, ill?

The last example showed a cleaner, sweeping the dust under the carpet. As she lifts the corner of the carpet, there's a sign attached to it which tells her she's fired. That could translate into a story almost as it is, or you might want to think of other ways an employer might try to trap somebody who isn't doing their job properly.

Whether they succeed, or end up being tricked themselves, is up to you.

From now on, don't just laugh at jokes and cartoons. Cut out any interesting ones and add them to your ideas file.

Lists

Lists are powerful tools to use in short stories as they can reveal a lot about somebody's character.

For example, a slim, health-conscious vegetarian would have a very different shopping list to a working mum who doesn't have time to cook meals from scratch.

Simply listing the contents of somebody's pocket or bag can also provide a snapshot of that person's life and interests.

What can you glean from the owners of these two very different lists of items?

A small packet of tissues, a nose spray, a pack of painkillers, two plasters in different sizes, a safety pin, a plastic bag.

A lipstick, a mirror, face powder, blusher, mascara, hairbrush, comb, spare pair of tights.

The first list might belong to a hypochondriac, or somebody suffering from a bad cold, or simply a person who likes to be prepared for every eventuality.

The second list could belong to somebody who cares what they look like (most women would carry at least some of these items) or a woman who doesn't usually wear make-up who is on her way to an interview and needs to be sure she looks her best.

Lists can also lead directly to stories.

The following story was published in *Woman's Weekly* and later in the short story collection, *Making Changes* (published by Bridge House). You will notice that it has been written from a man's point of view (see *Sex Change*).

THE BLUE LIST

1 – Give up smoking
2 – Stop eating so much junk food
3 – Help an old lady with her shopping
4 – Drink less beer
5– Watch less TV
6 – Meet a nice girl and go steady

It was 7.30 on New Year's Eve. I'd just finished a frozen pizza. One of the soaps was on TV, I wasn't sure which one.

I turned the piece of bright blue paper over in my hand.

Last year's resolutions made in an after midnight haze. Most of them made sense, but help an old lady with her shopping? I had no idea where that one came from.

I had achieved none of them. I managed without a cigarette for exactly one hour. A year on and I was still eating the same diet of pizzas, burgers and take-aways, still a slave to the one-eyed-God, as I called the TV.

I found the list as I rummaged in a drawer looking for a piece of paper on which to scribble this year's list. All at once, there didn't seem to be much point.

I was nearly thirty. Still on my own, living in an easy to care for flat, conveniently situated ten minutes from work and five minutes from a fish and chip shop.

Worst of all, I still had no steady girl in my life.

Most of my friends were married, or much younger than I was. One or two were divorced and already embarking on their next serious relationship. The sudden realisation came to me - I was in a rut. Self pity was about to take hold when the telephone rang.

"Hi, Nick, it's Dean. We're all going to the Black Horse tonight. It's got a bar extension till 2 a.m. Better than the Royal Oak, eh?" I muttered something and he went on. "Are you going?"

I found myself saying no. "I'm not in the mood. I'll catch up with everyone later."

As I put down the phone, a man on the local news was rabbitting on about the New Year, saying it was a time of opportunity, a time to change, to start over. I looked at my long forgotten list and was filled with a determination to do better this year. I decided to start by tackling one of last year's resolutions before I thought about making any new ones.

I searched everywhere for a pin but all I could find was a fork. I spread the blue paper on the table, smoothed out the creases, then closed my eyes, and stabbed the list with the fork. It landed on Number 2 - eat less junk food.

I sighed and went to the fridge. A few cans of beer, some lemonade, a pint of milk, a pack of Flora, some Dairylea and half a loaf of white sliced bread.

The kitchen cupboards revealed eleven tins of baked beans, a dozen packets of pot noodle, a packet of spaghetti a year past its sell by date, three tins of soup, some cream crackers (stale), a jar of Branston, two opened jars of pickled onions (great with fish and chips), six jars of peanut butter (two smooth and four crunchy), and an almost empty jar of marmalade.

There wasn't a piece of fruit or a vegetable to be seen, unless you counted the baked beans.

It was still early. I could go to the supermarket, and still get to the pub at a reasonable hour.

I grabbed my coat and set off. If I bought loads of proper food and filled up the fridge with fresh vegetables, I could start the New Year happy. If it was there, I'd have to eat it. Wasting food wasn't in my nature.

It was strangely quiet at Tesco, presumably people had already stocked up for the siege.

Instead of taking my usual sharp right turn and heading toward the frozen pizzas, I went straight ahead into the uncharted waters of the fresh fruit and vegetable aisles. I had no idea what I was going to buy.

It wasn't that I didn't know how to cook; when I lived at home, Mum insisted I took my turn in the kitchen along with my sisters. It's just that *everything looked 'difficult.' Why bother to peel a potato when you can buy chips, or slice up carrots when you can pop a frozen pizza in the oven, or better still, microwave a curry?*

A small voice behind me broke my train of thought. "Excuse me young man, could you fetch me down a bag of Satsumas? I can't quite reach."

"Of course," I said as I smiled down from my six feet two at the old lady who'd appeared, silently at my side.

"Thank you, young man," she said, as she disappeared down the aisle.

I thought no more of it until I reached the checkouts. Just in front of me was the same little old lady. I hoped she had a car. Her bulging bags looked awkward and rather heavy. Resolution number four popped into my head, but I'd helped her already by getting a bag down off the top shelf.

I unloaded my few purchases on to the conveyor belt. I'd decided not to go mad, just buy a few things to give this new way of eating a chance - some jacket potatoes (easily microwaved), a packet of sausages, some carrots, two large onions, two pints of milk, a loaf, and three bananas.

As I stepped outside into the already chilly night air, I almost bumped into the old woman. She was standing under the shelter looking to left and right. "Are you OK?" I asked her.

"My granddaughter's meant to be picking me up. Only she's not here."

It wasn't my problem, the granddaughter would be sure to turn up soon, but then that blue list popped into my head. "Where do you live?"

She gave me an address, not five minutes from my own flat.

"If you like, I could give you a lift."

"I'm not sure. Fiona might spend ages looking for me."

"Has she got a mobile?"

"Yes."

"You can call her - say you're on your way home. She can meet you there."

The old woman peered at my bright yellow phone. "I've never used one of those. Can you do it for me?"

There was no reply, so I left a message, telling a woman I didn't know that I was giving her Gran a lift home. "I left a message. Is that OK?"

She said it was, so I helped her into the car, put her bags in the boot, and took her home.

As I drove, she hardly stopped talking. I found out her name - Mrs Adams, how old she was - 85, and loads about her granddaughter - Fiona, twenty-six, recently divorced, no children, librarian, and that they were spending the evening together, sharing a meal and some red wine.

She was still chatting as a key turned in the lock.

A young woman walked in.

"Hello, Fiona. This is Nick. He gave me a lift, and helped me with my shopping."

"I left a message on your phone," I said as I put the last tin away and turned to leave.

"I didn't have my phone with me," she said, giving her Gran a glare.

"But she said..."

Before I could finish the sentence, the girl turned to the old lady. "You've been up to your tricks again, haven't you?"

"Maybe," she replied with a grin.

"I'd best be off then," I said, not wanting to get involved in a row.

"Don't go," said Mrs Adams. "It's New Year's Eve. We could use some extra company."

"Now stop that, Gran. I expect Nick has people waiting for him."

As she spoke, I thought of Barry and Jim, Terry and Mike. They'd be well into party mode by now. "I'm meant to be meeting my mates, down the pub," I said.

"You don't sound keen. Do you HAVE to go?" asked Mrs Adams.

"No, I don't have to," I agreed.

Fiona took her Gran's hand and squeezed it between hers. "Let him go to his friends. He doesn't want to spend New Year's Eve with an old woman and a bookworm."

I started to say something but Fiona was still talking.

"This is the fourth time you've gone to the supermarket and come back with a strange man. I've told you so many times before, I don't need your help finding a date. Besides, it could be dangerous."

Mrs Adams raised her hands in mock surrender. "I'm sorry, dear, but I just can't help myself. A lovely young girl like you shouldn't be spending her time all alone."

"I'm not alone, Gran, I've got you."

"Goodbye, then," I managed to say at last.

The girl turned to me and sighed. "Look, you can stay if you like. I don't mind. We've got way too much food as usual." She glared at Mrs Adams, but the warmth was there for all to see.

I didn't protest again. To be honest, the appeal of the Black Horse had faded the moment I saw Fiona.

She reminded me of a pixie. She looked small, delicate, although as she stood close to me I could see she was easily five feet six, maybe more. Her grey eyes danced with life and mischief. I got the feeling that being round her could be fun.

I was right, it was the best New Year's Eve I ever had.

The food was delicious.

We played games I'd only ever heard of before - Cluedo and Pictionary. I was hopeless, but it didn't seem to matter. My sides ached from laughing so much.

As we played and talked, I watched the two of them together, sixty years apart in age, but so close in other ways. Their love for each other shone like a star, so warm it even reached my cold heart. Fiona opened a bottle of Rioja and as the chimes of Big Ben rang through the house, we drank a toast to the New Year. 2004 was no more.

"Aren't you going to share a New Year kiss?" demanded Mrs Adams. "It's traditional."

Fiona raised her eyebrows. "Best do what she says, or I'll never hear the last of it," she laughed.

As I bent my head to kiss her, she slipped an arm round my waist and pulled me closer. I wanted that kiss to last forever, but it was over in a moment.

As we drew apart, Mrs Adams prodded me in the back. "Now be off with you. It's time I got to my bed."

I reached into my pocket for my diary. "Give me your number and I'll call you, that's if you'd like me to."

"It's 263116," said Mrs Adams.

Fiona laughed out loud. "Gran! I do know my own number! What if I didn't want Nick to call me?"

But I could tell by the way that she said it, that she did want me to.

As I got into the car and started the engine, a thin veil of frost was already forming. The two of them were still laughing and chatting as I pulled away.

It was a strange feeling, arriving home with a clear head. The night was so still. I felt oddly contented as I unloaded my shopping. Inside the flat, the blue list was on the table where I'd left it. As I read it, I smiled.

I was sober. I hadn't had a cigarette for six hours (a record for me when awake). The fridge contained at least some good, wholesome food. I'd helped an old lady with her shopping. The TV was off, and best of all, I'd met the nicest girl in Devon, who seemed to like me as much as I liked her.

As I drifted off to sleep, I decided not to make any new resolutions. Last year's would do just fine. After all, I only had one more to tackle, and that was half done already.

I hope you can empathise with the hero of that story. I know I can. I've written plenty of lists of resolutions that I fully intended to keep, only to find that by February 1st I've already broken, or forgotten, most of them.

There are other kinds of lists too. One that's come to prominence recently is the bucket list. That's where somebody writes down all the things they want to do, or places they want to go, before they die (or kick the bucket).

Exercise

How many different reasons can you think of that might make somebody write their own bucket list?

I'll give you a few suggestions at the end of this section.

Lists crop up all over the place, but we don't always notice them.

Here are a few more you might like to think about.

A list of guests to any kind of party. Such lists have conflict built in to them – who to invite and who not to invite. For example, what will happen when Uncle Jack meets Aunt Jane at a christening if they haven't spoken to each other for ten years following a row?

An inspector (MOT) or driving test examiner will have a checklist and if you're unlucky will give you a list of reasons why they have failed you.

A present list for a wedding, a baby shower or for Christmas.

A list of ingredients for a cake, or other recipe. Here you might start each new section with a different ingredient that relates in some way to the unfolding story.

As mentioned already, shopping lists reveal character – ready-meals as opposed to a joint of meat, branded products or the supermarket's own; these all tell us something about the person doing the shopping.

A list of pros and cons can make another excellent starting point. Once again, there is conflict already built in due to the for and against aspect of such a list.

Some reasons why such a list might be used could be deciding whether or not to move in with somebody, getting a pet, moving house or changing jobs.

I know that when I write a list of pros and cons to help me make a decision, I usually have a very good idea of what I want to do. I just want the list to confirm that decision for me, but what if the cons were twice as long as the pros? If that was the case, why might somebody choose to go ahead?

The obvious answer to this question is love.

If pet owners only looked at the downside of keeping a dog – vet bills, responsibility, mess, hairs, sadness when they get sick or die, bruises when they bash into you, etc etc, – they would never take the plunge, but they do, because on the pros side is that all important word, love.

It's the same with having children (or so I'm told!).

Now for some possible reasons why a person might decide to write a bucket list.

- The end of a relationship
- An escape from death
- Recovery from illness
- Loss of a close friend or family member
- Redundancy

Each of these could make somebody want to take stock, or make changes to their way of life and would be a good starting point for a short story.

Magazines

To me, magazines are like little books of ideas. There are the adverts that we looked at earlier, first lines of stories and articles, as well as photos and illustrations.

Many magazines also have letters pages where readers seek advice, offer solutions to problems, vent steam, or relate funny incidents. Any one of these can provide an idea.

If you want to write crime stories, or stories with a dark or violent edge, you don't need to look any further than magazines such as *That's Life*, *Chat*, and *Take a Break*. Within their pages, you can find everything you need.

I took a magazine at random and found these features, which would all translate fairly easily into fiction.

A husband, with eight children, who loses his wife and has to learn how to become a father.

A mother who is happy when her son finds love but before he has time to enjoy it, he dies. His fiancée, devastated by grief, commits suicide.

A man falls for a woman he meets at a bar and falls in love. They get engaged and plan to marry but she falls ill. Her last wish is to be buried in her wedding dress and for the groom to wear his wedding suit.

A true crime story about a man and wife. When the marriage hits the rocks, the husband murders his wife.

A double page spread told of children living in fear, and of the role of social services as they try to help them. There were several stories lurking in that one piece.

Fillers can provide ideas too. These are the small pieces of writing, often less than two hundred words that magazines use to fill gaps in their pages.

There aren't just horror stories either. If you look hard enough, you will find uplifting ones too.

In one of the fillers in that same magazine, a mother talked about losing her son. She followed his wishes, and his organs were donated to various people, saving four lives. This inspired her to raise money for charity in his memory.

I also found a feature about a woman who, when she was at school aged fourteen, was attracted to a boy but was never able to do anything about it because her friends didn't approve of him. When he kisses her at the school dance, she is so surprised, she runs away, back to her friends. Later, she leaves school and loses touch with the boy.

Years later, they meet by accident shortly before the woman is due to get married, but instead of going off with him, she marries another man. It's not until another six years have passed and her marriage is over that she finds him again on Facebook and the happy ending is finally reached. If that isn't a short story, I don't know what is.

Many of the cheaper, weekly magazines (*Chat*, *Best*, *That's Life* etc) are full of stories like this. All you have to do is find one that appeals to you and write it your own way.

I suggest choosing a magazine that you wouldn't normally buy. For example, if your magazine of choice is *Woman and Home*, try buying one of the very inexpensive weeklies like *That's Life*, *Pick Me Up*, or *Best*. That will make it easier to regard the magazine as a source of ideas, and not something to read for pleasure.

It will also expose you to different lifestyles which can be very stimulating and help prevent you from writing about the same kind of people all the time.

Memories

Children often don't understand the world the way that adults do. I'm thinking of that passage in *Cider with Rosie* where the boy is told to sit there for the present and gets upset when no present actually appears. It's a simple and obvious mistake.

A child's take on even mundane events can give them much greater resonance. You might think that stories written from a child's point of view would not go down well with adult readers, but this is not always the case. Magazines like *The People's Friend* often feature stories written this way.

Think back to your own childhood. Can you recall any times when you grabbed hold of the wrong end of the stick?

If you were unlucky enough to have parents who got divorced, do you remember how you felt? If you do, why not write a story about it?

Most people's memories are seldom perfect which means that if two people went to the same event, their memories of it may be quite different. This makes for a ready-made story, told from two viewpoints where it's obvious (to the reader) that one or both of them has got it all wrong.

This one idea can give you several stories. They can be sad or funny, sweet, or even nasty, according to your taste.

Take a couple; one who looks back through rose-tinted spectacles and their partner who remembers the bad bits too. How does that work for them?

Sudden memory loss, or what I call convenient amnesia, is a very well worn theme in fiction and is probably best avoided. For me, it seems that bit too convenient as a plot device. That said, it worked brilliantly in films such as *The Long Kiss Goodnight* and *The Bourne Identity*, so it can be done successfully. You just need to take care.

If, like me, you have problems remembering the past, old photo albums are great places to seek inspiration. A quick flick through, and all kinds of memories will start to come back.

If none of them prove suitable fodder for fiction, you can always try a nostalgia piece instead. There are plenty of magazines that are looking for that kind of writing – *Yours*, *Best of British*, local magazines and so on.

A visit to a local museum can also help you to recall things, but the best way is to start writing a diary, or an online blog. Then, when ten years have gone by and you want to set a story in 2010, you can consult your old diaries and be transported back in time.

As always, I have a word of caution for you. Remember that just because something is true, or actually happened, that does not necessarily mean that it will work well as fiction (see *Your Own Life*).

Newspapers

Newspapers have already been mentioned a few times, but I'd like to briefly talk about local newspapers again.

Being local, the stories covered are often more people-centred, rather than event-centred. In other words, you will find less about politics, celebrities and international affairs, and more about a man trying to break a world record for wearing the most hats/ underpants/gloves at one time.

These human dramas are tremendous fodder for fiction with the added bonus that if they are local, you may be able to go to the area to soak up the atmosphere. Then you can describe the scenery with the accuracy that actually being there can produce.

Newspapers often carry interesting photos that can be used to spark off ideas, or cut out and put in a file for future use as well as having pages of television listings, play and film reviews (see *Films*).

Several newspapers also have regular columns where a person writes about the ups and downs of life. Often these are ready-made stories. All you need to do is find a suitable ending.

Even crosswords can give writers ideas.

I've written two stories where the main character was struggling to finish a puzzle. In the first story which sold to *My Weekly*, the woman doesn't want the man to help her because they've had a row.

In the second story, which was published in *Yours*, the heroine is on a cruise with some friends. She is stuck on a clue concerning the seven deadly sins.

As the story progresses, each deadly sin is mentioned until one remains, and that is the answer to the missing clue.

Finally, there are the obituary columns.

Depending on the publication and the notoriety (or not) of the person who has died, these can be potted biographies of a whole life, perfect for basing a fictional character around. Even the smaller ones can set the imagination working.

For example, who is the person who keeps putting that 'in loving memory message' in the newspaper, year after year? We know it isn't the man's wife.

November 5th or Bonfire Night

This is another date with plenty of customs and traditions associated with it, any of which could provide the basis of a story idea.

Here are a few to start you off.

Collecting money for the guy. These days, it will take more than a few pennies to buy fireworks. Have you seen the price of rockets? What kind of money raising scheme could your character come up with?

People might gather together around a bonfire. As well as burning an effigy of Guy Fawkes, bonfires are often used to cook potatoes wrapped in foil and to heat up soup for the crowds that come to watch the fireworks. The traditional cake eaten on bonfire night is parkin, a sticky cake containing a mix of oatmeal, ginger, treacle and syrup. Other foods include sausages cooked over the flames and marshmallows toasted in the fire. There might even be a sing-song.

Thinking about fireworks again for a moment, what would happen if three people with very different views of November 5th are drawn together?

Bearing the current economic climate in mind, how does a single parent explain to his or her family that they can't afford fireworks this year? What happens if they pool their resources with somebody else?

Bonfires and dark nights are very atmospheric, which makes them ideal for spooky ghost stories. What if the guy is haunted? What other ghosts could be abroad that night, and why?

Then there are all the people (and animals) who are scared of fireworks. What do they do on November 5th? How might somebody overcome their fear?

Thinking about crime, which I confess I do quite often as it's such good fun, a large bonfire would be a perfect place to dispose of a body.

What if the guy looks so real because it is?

Nursery Rhymes

Like fairy tales, nursery rhymes have been around for a very long time.

Here are a few examples of some of the more popular ones.

- Jack and Jill went up the hill
- Old Mother Hubbard and her empty cupboard
- Little Bo Peep
- Jack Sprat, whose wife could eat no lean
- Little Miss Muffet
- Georgie Porgie, who kissed the girls
- Little Jack Horner, who sat in a corner
- Tom Tom, the Piper's Son, who stole a pig.

To find the story that most of these nursery rhymes contain, all you have to do is start asking those all important questions.

Why did Jack and Jill go up the hill? Was it really for water? Or was Jill married to Jack's best friend? How many times had they been there before the accident?

Why was Old Mother Hubbard's cupboard so bare? Did she have gambling debts? Did she give the last of her food to her no good son? What happens to the dog, that's what I want to know?

Who stole Bo Peep's sheep? Were they found again?

Did Georgie Porgie, the boy who kissed the girls, end up happily married, or is he still chasing girls at the age of fifty-two? Why did the girls cry when he kissed them? Was he terribly ugly or just have very bad breath? Or was he, in fact, a serial killer in the making?

Why did Jack Horner sit in a corner, eating by himself? Was he really a good boy like the rhyme says, or had he done something really naughty?

And what drove Tom to steal that pig? Is he a serial criminal, or are his family starving and relying on him to find food?

Any one of these could be turned into a story and there are literally dozens more.

You might not realise it at first, but many nursery rhymes have a dark side to them covering issues, such as poverty and overcrowding and sickness.

Quite a few also involve criminal activities of some kind. This is what makes them such a great source of ideas.

If you want to read an example of a story which takes its inspiration directly from nursery rhyme characters I recommend Neil Gaiman's story, *The Case of The Four and Twenty Blackbirds*.

Here he takes not one, but several characters and weaves them into a very convincing crime story. Little Jack Horner becomes a world weary private eye, and Humpty Dumpty is the murder victim. It's great fun and very well written.

One day, I was at a creative writing group and we were asked to take a nursery rhyme character and put them in a story.

I settled on Jack Sprat and his relationship with his wife.

This is what I came up with.

A two hundred word version of this story was published in an e-book of flash fiction by Spikethecat.

JACK SPRAT WOULD EAT NO FAT

Mrs Sprat looked at the chubby pink pig and chuckled with glee. "I can practically taste that bacon fat." She turned to her husband Jack. "It's time we booked the slaughter man."

But the next day, when Mrs Sprat went to give the pig its last feed, the barn was empty.

The police didn't find any signs of a break-in.

"That's because we don't bother locking the barn," Mrs Sprat explained.

"Who'd want to steal a pig?" added Jack.

"I have a shrewd idea," the police officer replied. "This sounds like the work of Tom, the piper's son."

"Surely not," replied Jack.

Mrs. Sprat nodded. "It makes sense, Jack. Remember when Tom was a lad? He stole a pig and ran away."

"But he's turned over a new leaf since he married Lucy Locket," Jack protested.

"Unless you have any other ideas," said the Police Officer. "I'll bid you good day."

When they were alone, Mrs Sprat sighed miserably. "I was really looking forward to some crackling."

Jack forced a smile. When they met, his wife's figure went in and out in all the right places. Now it only went out.

"Don't worry. There's still some cold beef in the fridge." Nice and lean, he thought.

Mrs Sprat turned up her fat little nose. "No, thanks. I'm not eating that. I want my bacon."

As she waddled away, Jack's heart ached. His friend, Dr Foster, had told him that unless his wife lost a stone in weight, she could die.

Jack had tried tempting her with lean meat, but she wasn't interested.

Two weeks passed with no sign of the pig. Jack sat down to his supper of lean roast chicken. "This is delicious. Would you like some?"

"No thanks. Obviously, our pig's gone forever so I'm buying one of Bo's lambs."

That same night, there was another robbery. It was all over the news.

'Last night, Miss Peep's entire flock of sheep were stolen. Police are baffled.' The scene cut to a weeping shepherdess. 'Who could have done this?" Bo Peep wailed.

Jack switched off the TV and comforted his wife. "I'm sorry, dear. That's your roast lamb gone. How about some low fat cheese instead?"

Mrs Sprat blew her nose, loudly, in a tissue. "I've hardly eaten a thing since our pig was stolen. I've lost more than a stone."

"That's wonderful news." Jack told her what Doctor Foster had said. "I don't know what I'd do if I lost you." He hugged her. "Our pig wasn't stolen. He's down at old MacDonald's farm with Bo Peep's sheep. I'll pick him up tomorrow morning."

Mrs Sprat smiled. "Leave him there, Jack. I went off fatty food ages ago. I thought you wouldn't love me if I lost weight."

"I'll always love you, fat or thin. Don't you know that?"

She kissed him. "I do now. Fetch me some of that nice low fat cheese, will you sweetheart? I'm starving."

As you can see, all I did for this story was think around the subject until an idea came to me.

I began by thinking about the difficulties that would be caused if a husband and wife had such different diets. That led me to dieting and issues about healthy eating.

In my story, I chose to take a light-hearted look at Jack's problem, which, when you think about it for a few moments, is quite a serious one. I could have used the same idea to write a much darker version in which Mrs Sprat dies because Jack is unable to help her.

If you are too old to remember nursery rhymes but think they sound interesting as idea prompts, you might want to visit this website where you will find dozens of rhymes, as well as all the words www.rhymes.org.uk. Almost all of them can be turned into stories.

Objects

Most of us have one or more treasured possessions, the things we would rescue first in case of fire.

Often these bring back memories of a special person or a time in our lives that was important to us.

Even if these objects were mass produced or worthless, they can mean the world to their owners.

Using objects to generate ideas can work well, providing you start to look at the object not as a thing, but as a possession. Once you do that, a story will often begin to appear.

I find that boxes are good places to start, especially ones with locks. Ask yourself who did the box belong to? Why did it need to be locked? Why does grandmother have love letters hidden away that were definitely not written by her husband?

If the box is empty now, what did it contain?

Stones, shells, feathers and other natural objects are also very good as starting points for poetry.

When examining an object, don't forget to use all the senses.

What does the object smell like? How does it feel to the touch? Does it make any sound? I'm not suggesting taste here for obvious reasons, although I did once take part in a class run by the romantic novelist Kate Walker. The objects she used were chocolates which was great fun, especially as we got to eat them afterwards.

Exercise

Look round the room you are in now and imagine it belongs to a fictional character.

What is the first thing you see?

Maybe it's an ordinary coffee mug, with blue and white stripes. Whatever the object is, ask yourself who it belonged to and why it was important to them.

This simple premise carried a whole series of television programmes, *Through the Keyhole*, where viewers had to try and work out whose house the cameras were snooping round. The fact is that every room tells us something about the person who lives there.

The clues are in the contents, the decoration, the level of tidiness or cleanliness, the amount of clutter and so on. It's a bit like pretending to be Sherlock Holmes and seeing what you can deduce.

Hopefully the object you chose will start to yield some interesting questions and even more interesting answers. If not, try a different object as mundane or as unusual as you wish.

Shoes are especially good.

There is a well known saying that to really understand a person, you need to walk a mile in their shoes.

This means that unless you actually live the life they are living, you cannot fully understand what makes another person tick. Some actors go so far as to wear appropriate footwear to help them get into character.

You can try this for yourself. I'm speaking to the ladies here. Put on a pair of the most comfortable, flattest, old shoes you own and potter about for five or ten minutes, noting down how you feel, then change into your highest heels. Do they make you feel different? How do they affect the way you walk?

You should find some significant changes. Gentlemen can try this too by first wearing your oldest, most battered, most comfortable shoes, then putting on your best pair, the ones you haven't quite got used to yet. Notice how different you feel.

If you see the actor David Suchet playing Poirot on television, look at his shoes and watch the way he walks. As soon as you see that particular way of walking, you know you are watching Hercule Poirot.

Next time you pass a charity shop, why not drop in and have a look at some of the shoes on display? Pick one up and imagine the kind of person who might have worn it.

Were they old, young, rich, poor? Look carefully and the shoe will start to tell you its secrets. Obviously, this works with other kinds of second hand clothing too as well as the shelves of bric-a-brac.

Whenever I visit somebody's house for the first time, I always take a look at their books. Just a glance can be enough to tell you about their hobbies and interests, and whether they prefer fiction or non fiction. The condition of their books also reveals whether their owner buys them for show, or to read.

The great thing about objects is that they are everywhere and virtually every one has a story to tell. All you have to do is listen.

Overheard Conversations

Eavesdropping is not only great fun, it can be a wonderful source of story ideas.

As we only get to hear part of the conversation, we can't help but start to make up the rest for ourselves.

These are a few that a friend of mine noted down over the course of a week.

"I wasn't there, but I know what happened."

"And ninthly..."

"It's all about blood and love, well I mean."

"I'm not into that kind of thing. Not at my age."

These all tell us something about the person who said them, plus they raise questions.

The one I like the most is "and ninthly". The person is either the world's biggest bore or so full of their own self importance, they are practically bursting.

I'd never come across the word before. Firstly, thirdly, perhaps, but ninthly! It's the kind of thing that nightmare AGMs are made of. I can just picture somebody having to sit there and listen to that speaker going on and on and on.

Journeys by bus, coach or trains are my favourite places to eavesdrop. Most of the time, people don't seem to realise that their conversations can be heard by the other passengers.

Whenever I hear somebody talking, loudly, on their mobile phone, I like to imagine what the person on the other end of the call is saying. I wonder whether they've heard it all before. Maybe they're also on a train going in the opposite direction as far away from the caller as they can get. That's the beauty of mobiles. You can say you're in one place when you are actually a thousand miles away.

If I can turn one of those overheard conversations into a story, suddenly those calls become far less annoying.

Other places where it's easy to eavesdrop are supermarket and post office queues, waiting rooms and restaurants, so even when you're going to the dentist, it pays to carry a notebook with you.

Photographs

Photographs can be found in all kinds of places – in albums, in books, on people's desks, in wallets, in newspapers and magazines, on billboards, and on postcards.

They're on the internet too. The website www.ingimage.com has literally hundreds of thousands of photos which people can buy the rights to, for use in various publications. The good news is that there's no charge for browsing.

If you want a photo of a man or woman so that you can visualise your hero or heroine, all you have to do is type in the word 'people' and thousands of photos will appear at your fingertips – a huge cast of characters ready and waiting to populate your stories. There are also photos of couples and groups where you can begin to figure out relationships, likes and dislikes.

And it's not just people. Every subject you could possibly think of is covered, so if you need a setting, you can find a photograph to help you get the details right.

It's time for another **Exercise**. Go through an old family album and find a photo of somebody you don't know very much about. You don't even need to know who they are.

Now look at them closely. Look into their eyes and ask yourself, what did they want in life, and more importantly, did they find it?

What does their expression say about them? Study their clothes and the way they are posing. Did they have a secret, something they didn't want anyone else to know?

I find it's easier to do this exercise when I have no idea who the person is, which is why I cut photos of interesting looking people out of magazines and keep them in a file.

If I tried to do this with a celebrity, it wouldn't work half as well, because the things I know about them would keep coming into my mind and prevent my imagination from working freely.

Photographs are also great memory prodders.

When I go somewhere new, I imagine that I will be able to remember what it was like a few days later, but that's not always the case. But if I have a photo to remind me, it's surprising how much more information I can recall.

Photographs of scenes work well too, which is why I keep old calendars. If a view is empty of people, I can put whoever I like into the scene. I might try one person, or a couple, a family or a criminal, until something starts to make a connection. Paintings work well too.

At the start of this section, I mentioned photos being found on somebody's desk. Which photos a person chooses to display can reveal a lot about their circumstances. A happily married man might display photos of his wife and children, whereas a divorced man might only have photos of his children.

What about somebody who has no photos of his family? Is that because he doesn't have a family? Maybe he feels that having photos on his desk would be too personal, or he prefers to keep his work and his personal life separate.

Similarly, if a man or woman carries somebody's photograph in their wallet or purse, you can be fairly sure they are close to them.

Again, why not see if you can subvert these basic ideas?

What other reason could a man have for carrying a photo in his wallet?

He might keep a photo of his hated ex-wife to remind him never to get involved with a woman again. He could be an off-duty policeman, carrying the photo of a missing teenager, or a middle-aged woman with a photo of the baby she gave up for adoption thirty years ago, or even an assassin with the photo of his next victim. What reasons can YOU think of?

Pick and Mix

If somebody says to you, "Think of an idea for a story?", it can be very hard to do. It can be difficult to know where to start.

I find that it's easier to come up with an idea when your choices are narrowed.

For example, if you are asked for an idea about a dentist who's worried about his weight, at least then you know where you're going.

One of my favourite ways of coming up with original ideas (when I don't feel like stealing a plot from a book or a film) is to dip into my set of little pots.

I have four of these, each one containing tiny pieces of paper, on which are written either characters, settings, problems or objects.

Let's take a look at each of these in turn.

Characters go into the first pot. These can be as general or specific as you like – everything from 'an old man' to 'a thirty-nine year old member of the Women's Institute'.

Some examples of the characters in my pot follow.

A bus driver, a bookshop owner, a keen gardener, a woman who has just retired, a single mother, a student, a pianist, a magician, a motor mechanic, a kitchen assistant, a teacher, a dog walker, a thief, a liar.

It's time for a word of warning.

I only put characters into my pot if I would be happy writing a story about them.

For example, politicians, nuclear physicists, spies and ballet dancers are four occupations I know nothing about so I wouldn't want to write a story about them. That said, I've never driven a bus (I don't even have a driving licence), but I can imagine what it must be like, which is why that one can go into my pot.

In the second pot are various problems or sources of conflict. Again, some examples follow.

Loneliness, coping with grief, miscarriage, boredom, lost love, rejection, retirement, insomnia, an unkempt garden, a discovered secret or a lost pet.

My third pot contains a setting. Again these can be as vague as 'inside' or 'outside', or very specific such as 'the last bus home', or 'the reptile house at London Zoo'.

The last pot has an object of some kind.

Again, some examples follow.

A ring, a pond, Brussels sprouts, a spider, a car, a salad, an umbrella, a key, a shoe, or a painting.

Some writers have an additional pot for kinds of weather (rain, wind, sunshine, sleet and so on), but I prefer to choose my own to either match or contrast with the storyline.

Once your pots are full, it's time for the fun to begin.

All you have to do is pick pieces of paper from each pot. You need to take two from the characters' pot and one from each of the others.

The task then is to create a story using the various components.

Sometimes the combinations can seem impossible. For example, you might end up with a dog walker, an artist, the cinema, Brussels sprouts, and insomnia.

At first that kind of selection can seem ridiculous and not worth pursuing, but it's often these odd combinations that produce the best results.

All you have to do is, yes, you've guessed it, start asking those all important questions.

In the above scenario, my first question might be this. How did the artist and the dog walker meet?

Maybe the artist has a commission. He's painting a portrait and has to do it at the sitter's house. Therefore he needs somebody to walk his dog.

Now I would decide which of the two characters has the insomnia problem. Let's say I chose the artist. That would make him or her the main character.

The next thing to figure out is how he solves his problem and what exactly does the dog walker have to do with it.

A simple answer could be that the dog walker also suffered from insomnia at one time but found that if he ate Brussels sprouts with his dinner, he slept like a log.

Okay, so that's fairly daft, and wouldn't make a story, but it's an idea that might lead to something else.

If that thread of thought doesn't lead anywhere, I might ask another question. Why does the painter have insomnia? Have they always had it? Is it the result of stress or unrequited love?

If that still doesn't lead to an idea, I give up, put the pieces of paper back into their respective pots and pick out a different set.

I can do this over and over again until I find a combination that works. Within half an hour, I'll have found something I can work with.

It's important not to give up too soon.

A combination might look ridiculous or impossible, but if you open your mind, a good idea might emerge. No matter how silly the idea seems, write it down. It may lead you to something better.

Don't worry if the first time you try this method you find it difficult. Like all of these ideas generating methods and exercises, the more you use them the easier it becomes. You simply have to practise.

There are many variations on this pick and mix method.

One of my favourites features every month in Writers' Forum.

It's called Paula Williams' *Ideas Square* where you roll a die to pick the elements of your story. There is a different theme for each issue and they're always great fun.

Plots (And Why It's Okay To Steal Them)

Many of the stories we know and love aren't original. They were stolen from other writers.

The best known example of a plot stealer is William Shakespeare, who happily took ideas from all kinds of source material. The Brothers Grimm were guilty too.

Plot stealing goes on today too with, rather ironically, Shakespeare's plays often providing the source material. For example, the musical *Kiss Me Kate*, came from *The Taming of the Shrew*. Luckily there is absolutely nothing wrong with stealing plots. There are two reasons for this.

First and most important, because there is no copyright on ideas, only words.

If somebody took Act Two of *A Winter's Tale* and tried to pass it off as their own work, that would be plagiarism but if they took the plot and updated it, that would be perfectly okay.

The second reason is that because there are only a finite number of basic plots, we have no choice but to re-use them. How many there are is a subject open to debate.

Some people say that there are only seven basic plots. What these are exactly varies according to whose research you read.

One often quoted selection goes as follows.

- Man versus nature
- Man versus man
- Man versus the supernatural

- Man versus technology and machines
- Man versus self or the ego
- Man versus religion or God

Please note that I am using the word man here to denote the human race, it is not an indication of gender.

Another selection again names seven basic plots and goes into more detail about them.

You will notice that some match the first list, whilst others do not.

The Quest

Here the hero has to reach a far off goal and goes on a long and arduous journey to achieve it. A couple of obvious examples are *The Odyssey* and *Jason and the Golden Fleece*. A more modern version would be Tolkien's *The Lord of the Rings*.

Voyage and Return

This plot is similar to the Quest in that it centres on a journey made by the hero, the difference being that it involves visiting another world and then returning from it. One of the most popular films of all time fits this basic plot – *The Wizard of Oz*.

Other well known examples include the *Back to the Future* films and *The Lion, the Witch and the Wardrobe* by the great C. S. Lewis (sadly no relation).

Rebirth

This basic plot often involves enchantment with the hero seeking to break the spell.

One of my all time favourite films falls into this category. It's *Groundhog Day* where Bill Murray's character has to relive the same day over and over again until he learns to be a better person. Only then can he find true love.

It's A Wonderful Life fits this category too, as does Dickens' *A Christmas Carol.*

Comedy

I would not define this as a separate plot type myself as if it's funny, a quest, or a rebirth story could be called a comedy, but somebody somewhere said that comedy was one of the basic plots which is why it's listed here.

According to Aristotle, comedy portrays people as worse than they actually are, and tragedy shows them as better than they really are, which, when you think about it, makes a lot of sense.

Tragedy

Referring to Aristotle again, he defined tragedy as when an individual does things that lead to his own downfall. Basically, whatever happens has been his own fault.

Shakespeare wrote several tragedies. Of these, *Othello* and *King Lear* are obvious examples of how the hero brings about their own unhappiness. Othello does this by not trusting his wife, and Lear by rejecting his youngest daughter because she refuses to flatter him the way that his other daughters do.

Rags to Riches

In this kind of plot, the hero goes from having nothing to having everything they could possibly want.

Quite often, this success doesn't last very long and the hero ends up right back where he started. To regain their wealth or position, they may have to defeat an enemy of some kind.

The film, *Trading Places*, is one of my favourite examples. The Eddie Murphy character is plucked from the depths of the gutter to a life of luxury. To avoid going back to poverty, he has to team up with his one-time enemy to defeat the people who put him through all this. To confuse matters further, the film is also a comedy.

Several fairy stories fall into this category, for example *Cinderella*, *Aladdin*, and *Jack and the Beanstalk*. Dickens also used this basic plot in some of his novels. *Oliver Twist* and *Great Expectations* are two fairly obvious examples.

Overcoming the Monster

Here, the monster may be literally a monster as in *The War of the Worlds* and *Frankenstein*, or an evil person such as Hannibal Lecter in *The Silence of the Lambs*.

The monster may also be inside somebody's head. It can also be the weather or the forces of nature, as in several disaster movies (*Twister* is one example).

Crime stories where a detective engages in a battle of wits with a serial killer also come into this category.

In all cases, the plot involves the hero trying to find a way to defeat the monster. I particularly like the film *Tremors* (starring Kevin Bacon) where a group of people are terrorised by giant worms. It manages to be both scary and funny at the same time.

So there you have it, two versions of the seven basic plots available to writers.

There are various other theories but each of them has one thing in common – the number of plots they describe is strictly limited. If we couldn't keep reusing them, over and over again, we would have nothing to write.

Many people find the thought of borrowing other people's plots hard to come to terms with. It seems wrong in some way. If this is you, spend some time thinking about your favourite stories, books and films, and you will quickly see that they are all based on one of these basic plot ideas.

The fact is, there really is nothing new under the sun. As a writer, I find that very liberating.

Points Of View

The point of view a writer chooses can change the entire feel of a story.

Using the first person brings everything into closer focus. It allows the reader to enter the character's mind and hear their thoughts. It's often easier to deal with emotions this way as it makes them seem more real.

On the other hand, using the third person viewpoint allows the writer to take a step backwards and tell the story from more of a distance. This can be very useful where the plot is complicated.

Exercise

Why not have a look at any of your unpublished, third person, stories and see if they would work better told in the first person?

The reason I'm mentioning this here is that changing from first to third person viewpoint can alter a story so much, it may be enough to turn a reject into a success.

If you have taken the trouble to come up with a good idea, why waste it if you can recycle it instead?

Another trick to consider is writing the story from two different viewpoints and switching back and forth between them. This method allows the writer to show all the misunderstandings and uncertainties that make up people's lives.

We may assume that the man who has moved into the house two doors down doesn't want to be friendly because he's a snob, but if we hear his side of things, we might find out that there are other reasons for his reticence – a bitter divorce maybe. We'll never know unless we get to hear his version of events.

Postcards

I love postcards.

They're like mini snapshots of places and time. They're also readily available, take up very little room and are cheap to buy.

If I plan to set a story in a location I've only visited once or twice, I often turn to postcards to help bring back the memories more clearly.

Old postcards are also enormously useful if you want to set a story in the past.

Of course, postcards aren't always of wonderful views. Think of the funny, rather naughty, ones by Donald McGill. Often these showed a small man being bullied by his much larger wife, or 'misunderstandings' regarding buxom ladies. To me, they are like stills taken from a short film as they nearly always have at least a couple of characters, interacting in some way. This is perfect fodder for the short story writer.

Postcards can also be bought at museums and art galleries that depict works of art.

Exercise

Visit a gallery, and find a picture you can gaze into. Imagine you are there, inside that painting.

What else can you see that is not actually shown? What can you feel, smell, taste or touch? Make some notes then buy a postcard of that painting to help you work on the idea at leisure.

If your memory isn't one hundred per cent reliable, buying postcards whenever you visit somewhere new is a good habit to get into. Sometimes all a story needs to make it work is a sense of place. Staring at a postcard may be enough to help you find it.

Writing a story in the form of a series of postcards is another idea you might want to think about. I once read a story that consisted of postcards written home to his father by a vampire on his travels. It was so good, I gave it second place in the competition I was judging. I haven't seen another one written in that form since.

Why not see if you can think of an unusual character and send them off on holiday somewhere? Who would they send postcards to and why? You never know, a prize winning story may emerge.

Problems

Ideas for stories often start with a problem.

The problem may be very small, like having a bad hair day, or suffering from a cold, or it may be of catastrophic proportions, such as having been diagnosed with a serious illness or facing a hurricane.

Problems are something we never run out of.

We all face them every hour of every day. They may be as mundane as deciding what to wear, what to eat, or what to do next, but the fact is that every decision we make, everything we do, can be considered a problem when it comes to finding ideas for stories. So, from now on, when you find yourself having to make a decision, or when things start to go wrong, or you face some kind of difficulty, look on the bright side. There will be a short story in there somewhere.

A list follows of just a few problems a character might come up against.

Debt, unrequited love, unhappiness at work, domestic abuse, being overweight, having some kind of addiction, bereavement, illness, late for work, nervous at interviews, forgotten somebody's birthday, noisy neighbours, bullying, lonely, jealous of their sister or best friend, unable to have children, suffered a miscarriage, taken for granted by their family, learning a new skill like learning to drive or how to use the internet.

I could go on and on because there are literally hundreds to choose from.

One of the most fertile areas to find problems for your characters is that of relationships, not just with family and friends, but also with neighbours and people we work with.

Exercise

Choose one of the above mentioned problems and give it to one of your ready-made, stock characters. How might they deal with it?

It's time for another word of warning.

Take care that you do not allow your characters to solve their problems too easily. If you do that, you may have a piece of writing, but you won't have a story.

Stories emerge from people's struggles. If the difficulty they face is overcome at the first attempt, the story will fall flat.

For example, a woman who wants to find love might join an internet dating site. The first man she meets turns out to be her soul mate and they get married six weeks later. That won't make a good story because there's no tension, no ups and downs.

We need to see the woman struggle a bit more. Maybe the first man she meets seems nice but he's only after her money. She tries again but the second man she dates isn't interested in finding love. All he wants is company and somebody to cook and clean his house.

After this second disappointment, the woman almost gives up. It's only when she tries again that she meets somebody nice.

By the time this happens, the reader will have been drawn into the story and will be on the woman's side ready to celebrate with her when she does, eventually, prevail.

That's when you have a story.

Proverbs and Mottos

Most proverbs are actually tiny, self-contained stories.

For example, take 'A bird in the hand is worth two in the bush'. I can just picture the person, creeping closer to the birds hiding in the bush, trying to figure out how he can keep hold of the one he's already caught. As I think about it, it's almost like watching a miniature film.

Find a list of proverbs and go through them, and you will soon see what I mean.

The other wonderful thing about proverbs is that they often come in pairs that directly contradict each other.

For example, 'Absence makes the heart grow fonder' as opposed to 'Out of sight, out of mind'.

Or 'Many hands make light work' and 'Too many cooks spoil the broth'.

There are many more.

What would happen if one person believed that he who hesitates is lost, but their colleague friend or spouse prefers to look before they leap? As they try to follow their differing ways of seeing the world, you have immediately created conflict.

Let's look at some more well known proverbs and see what might come from them.

'An Englishman's home is his castle.'

This gives me an immediate picture of a house-proud woman who spends so much time taking care of her home, she neglects other things, or a man who rules his home with hard and angry words but who is meek at work, or somebody who locks themselves away and doesn't want to face the world.

'Ignorance is bliss.'

This takes me to a secret, and how discovering the truth changes things forever. Or to a man who can't read, who fears what would happen if he could because that would mean taking charge of his life.

'Two's company, three's a crowd.'

Here I can see two people having a cosy chat when somebody plonks themselves at the same table and takes over the conversation, or two friends who go to a club and only one of them gets asked to dance.

'Life begins at forty.'

I've used this proverb as a starting point several times. It could be about somebody dreading turning forty and finding out that actually, it's okay. Maybe somebody has reached fifty and is still waiting for their life to start. In fact, it's possible to argue that life starts at any age, it's all up to the person concerned.

To me, proverbs are an ideas goldmine. As always, if you want to find plenty more, an internet search will do the trick.

One site I found really useful is called www.phrases.org.uk. There you will find hundreds of proverbs plus lots of other sayings too. Books of proverbs can also be found in libraries.

Rewrites

The fact is, stories can be changed in so many ways.

You can tell the same story from a different character's perspective, or use another setting (faraway countries are often popular with judges) or try a different time in history.

You might think about switching the genre of a story by turning a romance into science fiction, a western, or a comedy.

As we've already seen when looking at fairy tales, there are a myriad of ways to tell the same story so when you do get a good idea, don't waste it.

Milk it until it runs dry, then milk it again.

I hate wasting a good idea. If I can make more than one story out of them, that's what I'll do.

For example, the fear of flying story that appears under *Fears and Phobias* was given another lease of life when I used exactly the same idea to come up with a different story.

The premise concerned two passengers on a flight, each pretending to either be scared when they weren't, or to not be scared when they were.

As you will see, the second version of the story uses the same idea, only this time the man is pretending to be nervous so that he can get to know the woman. She IS nervous, but it isn't because she's scared about flying.

The result is a totally different story which was published in *Take a Break's Fiction Feast*. That one idea earned me hundreds of pounds.

You never know, one day, I might even write a third version.

FEAR OF FLYING

Rebecca settled herself into her seat. It was only a short flight to London. The worst part, the waiting, would soon be over.

The aeroplane was filling up fast. She crossed her fingers, then glanced down the aisle. It wasn't that she didn't want company, but her nerves were already in pieces. If the seat next to hers stayed empty, it would save having to make conversation.

She was starting to think that her wish had been granted, when a man appeared. From his suit, she guessed he was going to London on business.

He put a small case into the overhead locker, then took his seat without saying a word.

When he pulled a book from his pocket, Rebecca breathed a sigh of relief.

"Are you all right?" he asked.

"Sorry?" she said.

"You sighed. Are you worried about flying?"

She couldn't help noticing the genuine concern in his voice and the warmth in his grey eyes. "Actually, I am a bit tense," she admitted. "Nerves."

Before she could explain any further, the man closed his book and explained how aeroplanes manage to stay up in the air. "Statistically," he went on, "it's by far the safest form of transport. Even safer than catching a bus."

"Yes, I know, but..."

He cut her off. "Is this your first time?"

"It is actually. How could you tell?"

He smiled. "Probably because I'm not that keen on flying either, even though I know it's perfectly safe. I'd much rather travel by train, but there isn't always the time, is there?"

"I suppose not," she said.

"My name's Peter."

"Rebecca." She turned away, thinking the conversation was over, but he had other ideas.

"It's only a short flight. I wonder, could we do each other a favour? We're both nervous. If we spent the time chatting, it might take our minds off things."

Her instinct was to say no. Company wasn't really what she wanted right now, but, and it was a big but, she never could resist anybody who asked for help.

Besides, what he said was true. The more minutes that ticked past, the more nervous she felt. Maybe talking to somebody might help her to relax.

"That would be lovely," she said.

Peter smiled and put his book away.

At that moment, a stern voice echoed through the aeroplane as the captain introduced himself and his crew.

"This is the bit that gets me every time," admitted Peter.

He nodded towards the aisle where two flight attendants had taken up their positions. As they went through the safety and emergency procedures, Rebecca noticed he was gripping the edges of his seat so tightly, his knuckles were white.

At last, they were ready for take-off. As the engine roared and the plane gathered speed, she reached out and put her hand over his. To her surprise, he grabbed hold of it.

As the plane titled and left the ground with a loud rushing noise, his grip tightened. Soon they were airborne, and Peter relaxed.

"That's the worst bit over," he said, letting go of her hand. "So, tell me a bit about yourself."

It seemed like no time at all when the captain's voice announced that they were due to land.

"Do you mind?" Peter asked as he reached for her hand.

"No, not at all," she said.

"Safe at last," he said as the wheels touched the ground. Once the aeroplane came to a full stop, he undid his safety belt. "When are you going back to Exeter?"

"On Thursday. It's only a flying visit."

191

He laughed at her unintended pun. "I'm going back then too. I wonder, if we're on the same flight, I'd be happy to sit next to you again, if it would help your nerves that is."

"Thanks. I'd like that. I'm booked on the 4.15."

"Great, so am I," he said. "I'll look out for you. If you like, we can grab a meal once we're back in Devon."

Later, as Rebecca climbed into a taxi, she was smiling. She should have told him that it wasn't flying she was nervous about, she was nervous about appearing on The Weakest Link.

She was on her way to the TV studio to take part in the show. Her stomach had been churning since she got the call.

Flying to London was her reward for being brave enough to face Anne Robinson. After filming, she'd booked herself into a hotel, the idea being to console herself with some shopping if she was voted off first.

She hadn't had a proper break since her husband died, almost a year ago.

She thought about Peter and wondered if he meant what he said about going out for a meal. If he did, she'd definitely say yes. It was time she started dating again.

On the other side of town, Peter was hoping he hadn't laid it on too thickly. The moment he saw Rebecca, he knew that he wanted to get to know her better.

He'd flown hundreds of times and wasn't at all worried about flying. To him, it was like crossing the road. He gambled that by pretending to be scared, he'd bring out Rebecca's protective instinct. Luckily, his plan had worked.

When he reached his hotel to prepare for his meeting, he called his secretary on his mobile. "Sandra, something's happened. I need you to shuffle things around a bit. I want to fly back on Thursday instead, and make sure it's the 4.15 flight. ......Why? It's been two years since my divorce. My kids have been nagging me to start dating again. I've decided to take their advice."

Senses, The

When we write stories, it's easy to concentrate solely on the things we can see.

That's understandable as vision is the most important sense as far as human beings are concerned. However, our other senses are just as useful when it comes to writing stories.

Sounds, for example, can be very atmospheric. Think of a peal of bells marking the occasion of a wedding, or a fire engine's siren. Both summon up pictures and connections in our minds which means they will do the same with readers.

Smells are also very evocative. Many people find that some smells – their father's aftershave, or a particular food cooking, or the perfume of a certain type of flower – have the power to transport them back into the past, bringing memories vividly to life.

As with sounds, smells form part of our shared experience. Most people will know what you mean by the smell of an orange, or the sound of a violin.

Shared knowledge and experiences draw people into fiction which means that writers can, and should, take full advantage of this.

Think about taste for a moment.

Imagine the taste of strawberries, chocolate, or whatever your own particular favourite is, and you will probably feel your mood lift. Now try thinking of a taste you don't like and see how that changes the way you feel.

Now try the same thing using touch. It's easy to imagine the cold, hardness of marble and the soft warmth of a sheep's fleece. It's as though we can't help ourselves conjuring up the memory of how those things actually feel.

It's like that old parlour trick – as soon as somebody says, 'Whatever you do, do NOT think about a big yellow balloon', we can't help but see one.

Starting a story with something sensory, that most people will have had experience of, can be a very effective hook. Readers will immediately understand what you are saying and that draws them in, forcing them to keep reading.

The following is an example from one of my published stories where I used the sense of smell to open a story.

The story was called *The Smell of my suitcase* and it was published in *Woman's Weekly*.

For the second time in a month, the smell of my brand new leather suitcase is making me cry.

It's perched on the back seat of the car; I can't help but see it every time I look in the mirror. I should have put it in the boot, but I didn't stop to think. I wanted to get away.

Hopefully, as you read that opening, the smell of leather came to your mind. That combined with the questions these lines raise works to make you want to find out what happens to this person.

Here are some more starting points that will achieve that feeling of connection with a reader.

- A baby's cry
- The sound of a seagull
- The crashing of the waves
- The smell of petrol
- The smell of newly laid tar
- The taste of lemons
- The taste of a vindaloo curry
- A baby's skin, how it feels and smells
- An animal's fur
- A nettle from the garden

These are all very common, sensory experiences that most of us will have at least some knowledge of. As with so many things, it's their very familiarity that makes them so powerful.

Exercise

Make a list of five sounds that bring back memories for you. What is it about them that is so evocative? If you struggle to think of anything, try music. Is there a song or tune that means something to you?

Now do the same with the other senses – taste, smell and touch.

Can you use any of these as a starting point for a story?

Settings

Settings are often the last thing a writer thinks of when trying to come up with ideas for their stories. They think about the plot or the characters first, but is this always the best thing to do?

A story with a strong sense of place can linger in the mind for years. I'm thinking of books like *Lorna Doone* by RD Blackmore, or Conan Doyle's *The Hound of the Baskervilles* where the moors play such an important role.

In the same way as happens when we use the different senses, many settings conjure up their own atmosphere without the writer having to do very much. Some obvious examples are cemeteries, fairgrounds, supermarkets, fish and chip shops, a deserted beach, a wood at night, a music festival camp site, a swimming pool at its busiest time, the top deck of a bus, and so on.

All of these carry with them a set of associations because settings are like shared experiences. As with how things feel, smell and taste, we hardly need to describe what a doctor's waiting room is like because people already know exactly what we're talking about.

If an idea for a story isn't working well for you, a change of scene can sometimes inject the life it needs. Even the most mundane plot might be lifted by switching the action to an outpost on Mars.

It can also be fun and very effective to subvert the setting. In other words, you might want to use a bleak, deserted setting for a light and funny romance.

Exercise

Make a note of as many different settings you have experience of. When you have at least twenty, write them on pieces of paper and add them to your file or settings pot (see *Pick and Mix*).

Sex Change

I am not suggesting that in order to come up with an idea for a story or a book, you check into the nearest clinic and have drastic surgery. It's a lot less painful than that.

All you need to do is find a story and change the gender of the main character. The story could be one that you have written yourself, or an older, more familiar tale. Obviously it won't always work, but you'd be surprised at how often in does.

For example, would Roberta Hood and her Merry Maids work as a book or television series? It might. Were there any female gladiators? What about a female version of Jack the Ripper?

As you have already seen, coming up with ideas is all about learning how to view things from different angles and perspectives, maybe doing something that's never been done before.

For example, presenters of successful wildlife programmes on television always used to be male. I'm thinking of people like Sir David Attenborough, Desmond Morris and Johnny Morris.

Then somebody decided to give the job to an attractive young woman for a change. Who knows how many new male viewers Charlotte Uhlenbroek and Dr. Alice Roberts have brought to natural history programmes? Quite a few I would imagine.

Let's consider, for a moment, the women's magazine market. This remains one of the largest markets for short stories available today.

You might think that all the stories these magazines contain would be written by female writers but this is not the case.

Take a look sometime and you'll see that several men also write for this market. A few hide behind a female pseudonym but there are some who use their real name, people like Steve Beresford for example.

Again, it's easy to assume that all the stories will be written from a female point of view, with a female heroine, but again this is not true either.

In fact, simply changing the gender of the main character(s) so that we see a situation from a man's point of view can turn a well-used theme into something different and much more saleable.

For example, there are lots of stories about women getting married – the preparations, the doubts, the nerves, but far fewer from the groom's point of view.

Still thinking of weddings, the mother of the bride is another very popular character. What happens if you change that? How about writing a story from the prospective father-in-law's point of view? Or from the best man's? Or maybe the chief usher, who is secretly in love with the bride?

At once you have something different, which is exactly what magazine editors are looking for.

Why are stories like this so appealing?

If you are a woman, ask yourself this simple question – would you like to understand the way a man's mind works? Of course you would.

The fact is, to most women, a story written from a male point of view is inherently interesting. This helps to explain why this kind of story regularly appears in many magazines including *My Weekly* and *Take a Break's Fiction Feast*.

Changing gender can inject life into all kinds of situations. Readers' letters to women's magazines may appear to all be written by females but when you take a closer look you'll see that some have been written by men.

I can't prove this, but I'm fairly certain that magazines get relatively few letters from male readers. This makes them unusual and because of this, they are more likely to attract an editor's attention.

The result? They end up being published and the writer gets another cheque.

As you will have realised, I hate to let a good idea go to waste.

By now, I hope that you feel the same way, so have a browse through your back catalogue of fiction and consider whether a quick sex change might be enough to resurrect one of your stories.

Songs and Song Titles

Song lyrics can be great sources of ideas but you need to be very careful if you want to avoid any repercussions.

By all means take inspiration from the words of your favourite song, but don't be tempted to quote a couple of lines in the middle of your story as you may be infringing copyright rules. If that happens, you could end up with a very hefty bill. It's fine to use the idea, but not the actual words.

When you start to listen to songs properly, it's surprising just how many of them have lyrics that tell a complete story. In such cases, a ready-made plot is literally sitting there waiting for you to come along and write it up in your own words.

When I was at Swanwick Writers' Summer School, a lady ran a wonderful workshop where song lyrics were used as the inspiration for stories.

One song she played to us was Elvis Presley's *In the Ghetto*.

I must have heard that song dozens of times but I had never paid very much attention to the lyrics. When I did, I was surprised to discover that the words form a complete, well structured story. It starts with a baby being born, follows that child through his life and eventual death, then returns to another baby being born, doomed to repeat the same cycle.

Another song we listened to that day was *Piano Man* by Billy Joel.

Again it was the first time I'd really listened to the words. I was amazed to find that the lyrics are full of miniature character sketches, any one of which could make the starting point for a story.

There's the piano player himself, the bar owner, the waitress, as well as several customers, all of whom have stories that are worth telling.

Just a couple of minutes thought produced several songs with similar potential – *The Boxer, Yesterday, The Carnival Is Over, Lola*, and going back a few decades, *My Old Man Said Follow The Van*, and *Memories Are Made Of This*.

The fact is, there are countless songs like these, songs where you can simply take the storyline and use it for the basis of your own idea.

As always, if you're not sure of the words, lyrics for thousands of well known songs are available on the internet. Just type the title into a search engine, such as Google, and wait for the results.

If you don't want to use the lyrics, you might want to concentrate on the title instead.

Fortunately, there is no copyright on song titles (or any other kind of title for that matter) which means you can use them in any way you want to. You can even use one as the title for your own story or book.

You might remember the Chris de Burgh song, *Lady in Red* which was a massive hit back in the 1980s. As I listened to it one day, I asked my favourite question, "Why?"

Why was she wearing red? That led me to wonder what happened when she wore other colours and it wasn't long before I had the bones of a plot.

This is the story that resulted from that simple question.

It was published in *Best*.

LADY IN RED

Proposal

It was going to happen tonight. Excitement raced through her veins. What to wear? What to wear on this wonderful special night. A night that would live in her heart forever.

Her fingers raced up and down the rail as though they were playing Chopin's Impromptu Fantastique. They danced, pounced, pulled out and pushed back until at last they paused for breath. It had to be red. It had to be bold, dangerous. It must cling. Inflame. Set his heart on fire.

She snatched the dress from its hanger, hugged it close to her heart and whirled round. The scarlet material floated round her like a mist. The dress was light in her arms. No weight at all. As it slipped over her head, the colour reflected back off her skin. Her flesh glowed with warmth. Energy flowed into her. She was no longer a woman. She was a goddess.

Tonight, Paul would propose.

Wedding Day

The cool ivory material enclosed her like the case of a pupa. Inside, the old Catherine melted away. As the formal hairstyle, perfume and make-up altered the outside into something magical, so the person that was Catherine also changed, grew, developed.

A whole new life waited for her, as unknown as terrifying as the sky must be to a caterpillar, as dry land to a tadpole. Mrs Ritchie. No longer Catherine Jones. That very day, a new woman would be born. From out of the pure bright whiteness, a wife would emerge like the first snowdrop on a cold dark January morning. She melted into the deep snow that was her wedding dress and let it consume her. Love and peace filled her. Life was perfect.

Divorce Court

It was her day in court. Her day to stand up and tell the world. Her fingers slid along the rail, probing, rejecting.

The jade dress pushed forwards into her hand. Green for jealousy. Green for the monster whose eyes she saw through. Rich deep green like newly cut grass, damp and deep enough to leave the imprint of bodies tangled in passion. "Doesn't she know? Should someone tell her? She looks pale. She must know."

But Catherine didn't know. She didn't know about Amy or Susan. Didn't know about Angela until she saw them, fingers touching, eyes joined together, heads bent stretching across the table to be a fraction closer. She wasn't supposed to be there. Last minute decision. Fate. Call it any name you please.

She put on the dress. Green was her colour. Paul said it brought out the auburn of her hair, made it glow like smouldering embers. Let him see her one last time in green. Green for go.

Then let him leave if he wanted to. She would not, could not, hold him any longer.

Mourning

Time passed unnoticed. Days lengthened, then shortened. Her heart lay cold inside her, wrapped in the dark, deep shrouds of black. The once bright display in her wardrobe gone. Black, brown, black, grey, black, all that remained.

Black. The only colour she could bear to wear next to her pale empty skin. What did it matter if the world thought she was in mourning. She felt dead. Unwanted. Cast off. No longer the fresh white bride of three years ago. No longer the loved one, the lover. How foolish. How foolish to think she could keep him.

The heavy black dress hung shapeless on her shapeless body. Darkness swamped her bones. Stark white limbs appeared shyly from sleeves. Is this what love does, eats and nibbles away at flesh, sucks dry the body leaving empty bone?

"You'll be fine. You're still young. Forget him." Voices, well meaning this time. As if forgetting would be easy. Just take him off like an old dress, squash him into a bin bag and leave him in a charity shop doorway. Then buy something new, something clean, bright fresh smelling. Slip it on and forget.

206

She held up a blue jumper and tried, tried to imagine herself inside it. It was impossible. The only colour she could bear to see was black. Paul had taken colour from her life. The jumper joined the rest, squashed into the Oxfam bag.

Dark shadows hung beneath her eyes, a mockery of the pale green shadow she used to wear above them. Make-up dried out in a drawer. High heels gathered dust in the back of the cupboard. Alone, she was invulnerable. Alone, she was safe. Safe from heartache. Safe from love.

Rebirth

Her fortieth birthday arrived unwanted. Cards lay unopened on the table. She went to work as usual, let the routine take over. That evening she left the office late, anything to shorten the long dark night that loomed ahead. She was forty. Forty and alone. Once home she sat, staring at the fire. The flames danced but they only pretended to live, like she did.

The doorbell rang. She ignored it. It rang again, echoing round the still and quiet walls. It rang a third time. Slowly, Catherine went to the door. Her brother stood on the step, his arms overflowing with pink roses.

"Happy Birthday, Catherine," he said, thrusting the bouquet towards her.

"I'm sorry, Matthew. I don't want them. Please go." She tried to push the door closed but his hand held the frame.

"Your parents have booked a table at Giorgio's." He grinned, his perfect white wide smile. "I'm your escort for the evening." He bowed extravagantly.

The old Catherine would have laughed. Laughed at the idea of Matthew as an escort. At the ostentatious exaggerated bow.

"Sorry, but no. No, thanks, "she said. Again, she pushed the door but his arm was in the way.

"Mother said I was to insist. We don't think you should be alone on such an important day."

"It's very kind, but I can't go. I've got nothing to wear." It was a lie. She had lots to wear. Only everything was black and shapeless.

"She said to give you this." He handed her a small package. "Can I come in while you open it?"

Curiosity melted her defences. Silently she waved her brother into the hallway as she opened the parcel. As the paper parted, she saw red. Her fingers tore the

207

wrapping. Inside was her favourite red dress. The one she wore the day Paul proposed. Her beloved red dress, thrown out with all the others, a year before. Taken to Oxfam, by her mother.

Inside she found a card. 'Wear this today, for me. Love, Mum.'

"I can't wear red. Not anymore." She expected him to ask why but he sat silent, the flowers draped across his knee. Catherine looked at the roses, at her mother's writing, at the feather-light material she held in her hands.

She remembered the day, so long ago now when she last wore red. Heads turned. Hearts beat faster. She remembered the warm glow. The feeling of love inside her. Remembered happiness, excitement, love. Remembered feeling young and alive.

"Wait here for me, Matt," she said. "I need to think."

She climbed the stairs to her bedroom, the dress held in front of her like an offering. Reverently she placed it on the bed. It glowed, turning the bed into fire. Eyes on the blazing redness, she tugged off her black shroud. Then, as she slipped on the scarlet dress, she felt its colour. Felt its energy.

Unsettled, she turned towards the mirror. A pink flush filled out her cheeks. Her stick thin arms no longer looked stark and hard. A softness spread over her as she melted into the welcoming redness.

She tried a smile. A thin drawn face grimaced back at her. She frowned at it. Scrunched up her nose, poked out her tongue. Suddenly she was laughing, laughing, laughing.

"I'll be down in a minute," she shouted.

As mentioned earlier, this story came about when I started to think how wearing different colours can affect people's mood. For example, I avoid wearing black as it reminds me too much of funerals and makes me feel heavy. I wondered why the woman in the song was wearing red and what would change if the colour of her dress was different.

To give the story the structure it needed, I brought the story round in a circle. At both the beginning and the end the heroine chooses to wear red. The colour serves to show the reader how she is feeling and leaves us with an optimistic view of her future.

Using a song title as the title of your story, especially when it comes from a popular, well loved song like *Lady in Red*, is a wonderful way to create resonance.

Here, resonance means striking a chord with the reader. By using something that is very familiar to them, in this case the title of a song, the reader immediately feels drawn into the story.

Try it for yourself.

If these were titles of stories, would you be intrigued enough to want to read any of them?

If so, which would you read first and why?

- *Blue Suede Shoes*
- *Bridge over troubled water*
- *Rocket Man*
- *My Way*
- *Last Waltz*

If the answer to that first question is yes, which I'm hoping it is, that will be because of the resonance that particular title has for you. You will choose to read the story with the title that has the most meaning for you.

Once you know about this effect, you can use it to your advantage.

For example, if you are writing a story for *The People's Friend* where most of the readership are elderly, using a title from a very old song, like *We'll Meet Again*, might well give you an advantage.

This can even help in competitions. For example, if you know that the judge loves Elvis Presley, using one of his hits as the title of your story is bound to attract their attention. Thanks to social networking, you can find out many people's likes and dislikes by checking their website or Facebook pages.

Songs can also be used in stories as mood indicators.

For example, if the main character is listening to sad songs as opposed to singing along to something upbeat, we don't have to be told what mood they are in. We can tell by their choice of music.

Another use for songs is to help establish a sense of time and place. Opening with a reference to a band like Slade, T. Rex or Alice Cooper will let the reader know that your story is set in the 1970s, whilst Oasis will take them to the eighties, Bill Haley & His Comets to the fifties, and so on.

Exercise

Make a list of the popular songs you would want to take to a desert island.

Now listen to each of them very carefully, or find the lyrics on the internet. Do any of them contain a ready-made story, just waiting for you to release it?

Television

Almost every programme shown on television can be used to help generate ideas. All you have to do is pick one and settle down to watch with your trusty notepad by your side.

Some of my favourite shows are quizzes. You might think that getting ideas from these is impossible, but think again.

Take *Eggheads* for example where a team of remarkably good quizzers take on members of the public. Is there any rivalry amongst the *Eggheads*? Which of them thinks they are the best? How do they get on when the cameras aren't rolling? Does CJ ever feel like murdering the ever-smiling Daphne?

I once wrote a story based on *Who Wants To Be A Millionaire?* A woman who gets on the show has to phone a friend. It was all about the relationship between the woman, her friend and the man they are both keen on. It was published in *Chat* back in the days when they published fiction.

Many people watch soaps. I used to be a fan but gave up watching all of them some years ago when the good humour of shows like *Coronation Street* was replaced by constant bickering and endless affairs. Ken Barlow might be a very nice man, but I found it hard to believe that so many strong, attractive women would give him so much as a second glance.

That said, if you enjoy soaps, they are wonderful for ideas generating simply because of the conflicts, arguments and tangled relationships that fill every episode. All you have to do is take one of the plot lines and put your own characters into the story and see how they react.

Television is also useful if you enjoy people watching but don't get out as much as you would like. All you have to do is pretend that you are spying on the characters and make notes of the phrases they say, the way they talk, walk, their body language and so on. I keep a separate notebook for this very purpose so that when I'm stuck for a way to express somebody's speech or body language, I can dip into it for inspiration.

Listening to different characters' dialogue (here, I find sitcoms particularly helpful) will help you learn how to make your own characters speak in their own, individual way.

Sometimes a phrase or a word is so powerfully attached to a character that a catchphrase is born. Say "Lovely jubbly" and most people will think of Del boy in *Only Fools and Horses* whilst the words "Don't panic!" conjures up Corporal Jones in *Dad's Army*.

These are obviously extreme examples but you will find, once you start to pay close attention, that most people have phrases or words that they say frequently. I often find myself saying "absolutely". I have no idea why.

You can obviously watch and listen to real people speaking and study them but this is hard to do without appearing to stalk them. The danger too is that while you are listening to what they say, you may not notice what they are doing with their hands.

That's the beauty of TV. You can watch the same person over and over again.

Exercise

Pick a character from one of your favourite shows and build up a profile about them.

What is it about the way they look, speak, dress, behave and walk that makes them different from other characters in the show? What problems do they have? Can you make one of these the basis for a story idea?

Themed Competitions, Finding Ideas For

I have run and judged several short story competitions in recent years.

Some of these had themes. I found judging those competitions quite hard. Why? Because far too many entries were broadly similar.

For example, I judged a National Association of Writers' Groups' last line competition. The last line went like this – "Nobody steals my pumpkin".

Unsurprisingly, around half the entries were about people growing prize-winning pumpkins. After reading six of these in a row, it's hard for any judge to remain fresh. That can mean that a very good story, on that well-used theme, can be overlooked.

This is a problem that is very hard to avoid. I like to think that I DID manage to achieve a just and fair result for that competition, but the similarity of many of the plot lines made that quite difficult.

Judges are only human. They like to read something different. Once you realise that, you can increase your chances of being shortlisted in themed competitions simply by coming up with an unusual basic idea as a starting point.

To do this, brainstorm (or mind map) round the theme.

For example, if I was writing an entry for the pumpkin competition, my first idea would be growing a prize winning pumpkin and somebody's efforts either to protect it or to steal it.

I would then try to come up with some other basic starting points. Some of these might be a story about a jack-o'-lantern, a magic pumpkin, or a woman whose nickname is pumpkin.

I would keep thinking until I was happy that I'd come up with something that bit different. For example, somebody dressing up as a pumpkin for a fancy dress party. I would then develop one of those into a story. The one thing I would definitely NOT do is write a story about a prize-winning pumpkin.

Why not is simple. If that was the first idea that came to me, it's likely to be the first idea that occurs to several other people too.

No matter how good a story is or how well written it is, I wouldn't want to risk its impact being lost because so many other stories were broadly or vaguely similar. So reject the first idea you come up with and use another one.

Another tip is to think of using a different genre, one that doesn't immediately spring to mind upon reading the theme.

For example, if the theme was lost love, most people will write a standard romance, maybe looking back over somebody's life.

Once you know this, you can gain an immediate advantage by choosing a different way to write your story. For example, you might choose one of these genres – ghost, horror, science fiction, crime or fantasy.

Your story would still be about lost love, but the character who has lost that love could be a cowboy, a ghost, a wizard, or even a robot.

Obviously you still need to produce a well written, well structured story, but you will have the immediate advantage of having produced something that bit different.

Another option is to subvert the emotion. Looking at lost love again, most stories will be sad or reflective so if you can write something using another mood, for example using humour or writing from the viewpoint of somebody who wants revenge may be all you need to make your entry stand out from the crowd.

Twist Endings

Stories that end with a surprise continue to be very popular with fiction editors because people enjoy reading this kind of story.

Think of that most popular genre of all, crime fiction. The most satisfying plots are those where, when the culprit is revealed, the reader reacts with, "Of course, why didn't I see that myself?"

This is the reaction you want to achieve when writing any story which has a twist at the end. It's all about laying down the right clues. It's not about surprising the reader by suddenly introducing little men from Mars or saying it was all a dream.

Some of the more obvious twists follow.

- A character you think is a man turns out to be a woman, or vice versa.
- A character you think is elderly, turns out to be young, or vice versa.
- A character whose gender you have assumed to be female because of the job they do, turns out to be male, or vice versa.
- The reader assumes, wrongly, that it's Christmas, or some other time of year.
- A character appears to be doing one thing, or having a certain role, when they're actually doing something very different. A well used example is the 'boy' who doesn't want to go to school who turns out to be the headmaster.

These twists work because people make assumptions all the time, we simply can't help ourselves. It's part of being human.

Exercise

List some occupations that you might normally expect a man to do, and another list of jobs that are more likely to be done by a female.

Some suggestions can be found at the end of this section.

Sport is another area where it's easy to get the reader to make an assumption about gender, so footballers, cricketers and rugby players might be assumed to be male, whilst netball players are female.

For our purposes, it doesn't matter that there ARE female cricketers. All we're doing is letting the reader make an assumption and as most people who play cricket are male, that's easy enough to do.

This works for hobbies too.

Most people who knit or sew are female.

Most people who do woodwork or metalwork are male.

This gender bias is all you need to be able to build a twist on.

Weddings also offer opportunities for twists.

It's easy to get the reader to assume that the woman preparing for a wedding is the bride when she's actually the mother of the bride or groom, or a bridesmaid.

Similarly, they can be made to assume a man is the groom when he's actually an usher, the best man or the father of the bride.

One of my twist ending stories follows. See if you can work out what the twist is before you reach the end. Having just read this section, you might find that you can spot the twist quite easily.

Once you get to the end, look back through the story afterwards and try to figure out why the reader might have been fooled.

SELF CATERING *(published as Holiday Makers in My Weekly)*

"Thank goodness we're here at last," said Katie to herself as she put down her suitcase with a sigh. The unpacking could wait. Right now all she wanted was a rest. The long hours of travelling had tired her out.

The flight itself wasn't so bad, once they were up in the air. In fact the time went fast enough once they got going; it was all the hanging about at the airport beforehand that really got to her.

Every airport terminal looked the same, it was only the language the signs were written in that changed. There was never enough to do, and the snacks were often overpriced and dull. For her, the travelling was always the worst part of a holiday. She looked forward to the days when people could just beam up like they do on Star Trek

She turned and glanced out of the window, wondering what was keeping Rick. The view wasn't up to much, just lots of houses and flats stretching away to the distant hills. It would be lovely to be right by the sea, but places with a sea view cost a lot more, and their budget wouldn't stretch to that at the moment. Maybe next year.

Katie glanced round the room and smiled approvingly. It all looked neat and tidy. The walls were painted in a subtle shade of blue, the kind of colour that wouldn't offend anyone. The large pine wardrobe didn't match the chest of drawers, which didn't match the bedside cabinet, but she didn't mind. There was lots of storage space.

After all, what do you really need in a bedroom? It wasn't as though they spent all their time there. As long as it was clean and comfortable, and there was enough room to hang their clothes.

She stood still for a moment and wondered what to do next. It was two thirty in the afternoon, the sun still high in the sky. A siesta would be nice. The Spanish had the right idea there. That was one European custom that Katie thoroughly approved of, especially as it meant the shops were still open late at night.

With a rueful smile, she wondered how many words of Spanish she'd still remember by the end of the month.

She decided to check out the bathroom before finding out what was keeping Rick. There were lots of lovely clean towels, a power shower over the bath, soap, bath oil and shampoo. Everything a girl could need in fact. With a happy sigh, she opened her case and pulled out her bag of toiletries. She plonked them down on the shelf, doing her best to ignore the pile of clothes that needed to be unpacked.

They'd have to go out sooner or later to buy a few bits and pieces - they'd finished the last of the bottled water on the plane t but right now all she wanted to do was sit on a chair that wasn't moving.

With a groan of relief, she pushed off her shoes and flopped down on the bed. There were lots of lovely plump white pillows and the bed was a nice big double one, not the twins beds they always seem to put in hotel rooms, especially in Spain.

She bounced up and down a few times but the effort was too much for her. She was tempted to shut her eyes and doze off for a few minutes, but Rick still hadn't appeared. With a sleepy yawn, she slipped her shoes back on and went to find him.

She found him rummaging through his hand luggage, a frown of concentration on his face. "What are you doing darling? I've been waiting for you in the bedroom." She gave him a mischievous grin.

"I hope you're joking. The journey's tired me out."

"You poor old thing," teased Katie. "So what are you looking for in there?"

"The milk we brought with us. I could murder a cup of tea."

"Men," said Katie as she slipped her arms round her husband's waist. "Always thinking about food and drink." She gave him a big squeeze. "Let's go out for a meal tonight. I don't think I could face cooking at the moment."

"That's not a bad idea," he said. "I don't know about you but self catering's going to take a bit of getting used to."

"Right, that's settled. We'll have a cuppa then pop down to the shop for some supplies. Then we can chill out in front of the TV until it's time to go out and eat. Shall I see what's on?"

"Why not," said Rick, holding up the carton of milk with a flourish. "I'll make a brew."

Katie turned on the television, then collapsed into the nearest chair.

Just then there was a familiar clanking sound as Bertie came flying in through the cat flap. He leapt on to Katie's lap with one bound and immediately began to purr like a train.

"I didn't think it would take him long to figure out we were back," laughed Rick.

"All inclusive holidays are wonderful, aren't they?" said Katie as she stroked the cat's soft grey fur. "But if you ask me, there's something even better."

"Getting back home again," they said together.

You are meant to assume that the couple are going away on holiday because that's how holiday stories often begin. You will have noticed that I talk about the journey and the disappointing view.

Again, this adds weight to the idea that the couple are at the start of their holiday. Once the reader has this idea in their head, they will apply it to the rest of the story.

As they read on, they will assume that the room the woman is checking out is her hotel room. Everything will be coloured by that simple first assumption that the couple have just arrived at their holiday destination.

Of course, that isn't the case; the couple have actually just arrived home again, AFTER their break.

Once you know that, you can look back through the story, and find that the clues are all there to see. Never once did I say they'd just arrived, or purposely lie to the reader in any way. All I did was mislead them into making the wrong assumption.

In a nutshell, that's the art of a twist ending story – all you have to do is get the reader to fool themselves.

Some possible answers to the exercise follow.

Stereotypical male occupations – doctor, boxer, lawyer, police officer, architect, dentist, surgeon, Managing Director. .

Stereotypical female occupations – nurse, nanny, typist, receptionist, secretary, babysitter.

Valentine's Day

Like Christmas Day, February 14th comes round every year.

Most women's magazines that publish fiction will carry at least one Valentine's Day story which means it's well worth trying to write an original story on this theme.

As with any seasonal story, Valentine's Day stories need to be written several months in advance. The logic is simple here.

Firstly, magazines prepare their pages months in advance.

Secondly, if a fiction editor needs three Valentine's Day stories and has already bought three, the next one that comes along is likely to be rejected, even if it's very good so I aim to start thinking about Valentine's stories in September or October at the latest.

Sadly, my life has been lacking in romance for too many years. If I had to wait for something romantic to happen to me before I could come up with a story idea, I might never do it.

So that I have plenty of starting points to work with, I keep a file in the same way I do for Christmas ideas. There I keep all kinds of romantic bits and pieces – Valentine's cards, articles about true love, plot outlines of films.

When February comes along, I read as many Valentine's stories as I can and add them to the file.

Once again, thinking round the subject is the best way to start to come up with possible ideas, so you might want to begin by making a basic list.

Exercise

List at least six things you might associate with Valentine's Day. As always, some possible answers are to be found at the end of this section.

An example of one of my stories follows. It was published in *Take a Break's Fiction Feast*.

TOO OLD FOR ROMANCE

It was February 14th, but Hazel Burroughs wasn't expecting any cards.

She was fifty-eight and had been a widow for ten years. As far as she was concerned, her chances of finding love and romance had long gone, so when she picked up the mail and found a pink envelope, festooned with roses, she couldn't help it, she gasped.

Then she looked at the address. Mr Derek Harding, 2A Petunia Crescent. The postman had made a mistake. Mind you, she couldn't blame him. The A did look a lot like a 4.

She glanced outside. It was grey and cold, but it wasn't raining. She put on her coat and shoes. It wouldn't take a minute to deliver the card herself. As she walked down the road, she couldn't help feeling more than a bit curious.

Derek had moved to the crescent six months ago, and as a single, older man, had been the topic of much conversation in the queue at the Post Office. He'd moved to the area after getting divorced. Immediately, Margaret Evans had set her sights on him, but he'd proved oblivious to her charms, refusing all offers of homemade dinners and cakes. Everybody assumed he preferred to be on his own.

Hazel wondered who'd sent him the Valentine. As far as she knew, he definitely wasn't seeing anyone. She glanced again at the pink envelope. Maybe Margaret had sent it.

When she reached 2A, she pushed the card through the letter box, then went back home.

She thought nothing more about it until the next day when she popped into the corner shop for a loaf of bread.

226

She met Derek on the way out. The moment he saw her, he smiled. "Hello, Hazel. How nice to see you. Lovely day, isn't it?"

"Yes, it is," she replied.

They chatted for a couple of minutes about the weather, and the latest happenings on Eastenders. "Well I'd best be off," he said at last. "Good day."

Hazel watched him leave. It had been one of the longest conversations they'd ever had. Normally she counted herself lucky if he said hello.

"What's got into him?" she asked Margaret when she got to the counter.

"Somebody sent him a Valentine's card."

"I know. The postman delivered it to me by mistake. I put it through his door. I thought you'd sent it."

Margaret laughed. "No. It wouldn't do me any good. I've already asked him out three times. He politely, but very firmly said no. Apparently, I'm not his type, more's the pity."

"I wondered if it's anyone we know," mused Hazel. "He certainly seems happy. Maybe he's in love."

As she spoke, she felt that unfamiliar feeling again, what was it? Jealousy? She pushed the thought from her mind. She was pleased for Derek. He was such a nice man. He deserved to find love again.

Suddenly she noticed that Margaret was grinning. "What's wrong? Why are you looking at me like that?"

"Derek's convinced the card was from you. He saw you put it through his door."

"Oh, dear. I didn't think of that."

"What are you going to do?" asked Margaret.

"Tell him of course. I'll call on him, tomorrow afternoon, on my way back from the library."

The next day, as she reached Derek's gate, Hazel was deep in thought. By admitting that she didn't send the card, she was leaving the way open for whoever it was who HAD sent it. She was thinking about turning back, when the front door opened, and Derek called out to her.

"Hello, Hazel. I was just thinking about you." She noticed the twinkle in his grey eyes, and couldn't help smiling. "If you've got a moment, why don't you come in? I was just making a pot of tea."

227

She walked down the short path, but then hesitated on the doorstep. Her conscience was prickling away at her. She needed to tell him the truth before she lost her nerve.

"I'd better not. This is awkward for me, Derek. I need to talk to you about the Valentine card."

"Yes, I'm sorry about that. I'd never have guessed it was from you. I just happened to be looking out of the window when you popped it through the letter box." He grinned. "I was very flattered. It perked me up no end."

"The problem is, it wasn't me who sent it." She explained about the postman getting the address wrong.

"Oh, I see. Silly me. I should have realised something like that had happened. Sara must have sent the card. She's got terrible handwriting."

Hazel wondered who Sara was, and why she felt so jealous, and even more puzzling, why Derek sounded so disappointed. "Sara?" she echoed weakly.

"Yes, my niece. Lives in Northampton. Ever since I got divorced, she's been nagging me about dating again. Oh well, never mind. It was good while it lasted."

Hazel didn't know what to do next. It seemed she didn't have a rival after all. What's more, Derek had definitely seemed pleased when he'd thought she'd sent him the card.

"About that tea," she said. "If the offer's still open, I'd love a cup."

Derek smiled warmly and beckoned her inside. As the front door closed behind her, Hazel couldn't help thinking how lucky it was that the new postman had made that mistake.

An hour later, as she sat on Derek's sofa, holding his hand, she realised something.

She'd been wrong. Fifty-eight wasn't too old for romance after all.

The idea for this story came to me because, at the time, my house number was 2A and I did sometimes get the wrong mail.

All I had to do was imagine some of the complications that it might lead to.

I started out thinking about boring things like bills and bank statements, then on to Christmas and birthday cards, before landing on the Valentine's Day angle.

You will notice too that the heroine in my story is in her fifties.

Love, thank goodness, isn't confined to people under thirty-five. So when you're thinking about Valentine's Day stories, you might want to give some thought to the age of your protagonists.

It's easy to write about people who are of similar age to ourselves. Many people find that they do this all the time, almost without thinking.

If this sounds familiar to you, why not make a point of writing about somebody who is twenty or thirty years older (or younger) than you are and see what difference that makes?

Another way to come up with a saleable idea is to subvert the whole romantic angle.

For example, the heroine is delighted to receive post on February 14th but it's not a card she opens, it's her long awaited decree absolute.

Maybe you could mix up the genres by writing a ghost or crime story where the action takes place on Valentine's Day?

When trying to sell short stories, it helps to try something that bit different.

Each year, when February 14th comes round, fiction editors will be swamped with dozens of lovey dovey, slushy stories.

If you can send them something rather more unusual, your story will be the one that gets noticed. It really is as simple as that.

Some answers to the exercise follow.

Valentine cards, shop displays of soft toys, special meals, bouquets of flowers, boxes of chocolates, champagne, soppy films, engagement rings, weddings and marriage proposals.

What If?

This method of generating ideas couldn't be simpler. All you do is take a situation and ask, "What if?"

For a romance, try these. This one is for the ladies. What if Brad Pitt/George Clooney/Sean Connery came to your office, took one look at you, and fell head over heels in love? What if you were so attractive, men were always asking you to marry them?

And now for the men, what if your wife wasn't there when you got home? How would you persuade her to come back to you?

For a ghost story, any of these might work. What if ghosts were everywhere and you were the only one who could see them? This idea was used to great effect in the film, *The Sixth Sense*. Or what if a ghost took up residence in your car/office/corner shop/pub?

For something more domestic, you could try these. What if your child's teacher was in a wheelchair? What if a stranger gave you a ten pound note? What if you fell apart at interviews?

"What if?" can be applied to more or less anything you can think of. It's especially good for science fiction or fantasy.

For example, you might ask these questions. What if you could fly? What if all the electricity in the world suddenly stopped working? What if you could read people's minds? (As in *What Women Want*, starring Mel Gibson)

You can have enormous fun with "What if?", and if you keep asking questions, you will find that stories start to emerge with very little effort on your part.

Writer's Block

My opinion of writer's block is simple – if you believe it exists, then it does.

Sitting, staring at a blank sheet of paper can be stressful, especially if you only have a limited time in which to write. The pressure to produce something can be very high.

Personally, I don't believe in writer's block and have never suffered from it. That's not saying that I can write brilliant stories all the time. Quite often the words that come out aren't very good at all, but I know that so long as I keep writing those words, sooner or later something useful will emerge.

So here's my cure for writer's block.

Take up your pen and paper (or sit at the keyboard) and start writing.

It doesn't matter what the words are. If you can't think of anything, jot down your thoughts about life or describe the room you're in, in as much detail as you can. Soon, other more useful thoughts will start to creep into your mind.

When you first try this, it might take a while before anything starts to happen, but happen it will and the more you practise the technique, the easier it will get.

The other trick I use when I'm stuck halfway through a story, or can't think of the right ending is to stop writing, and go and do something else.

My favourite activities are gardening or baking as they occupy your mind as well as your body, but going for a walk, doing a jigsaw, even calling somebody on the phone, may work just as well.

Before very long, new ways to take the story start to come to me simply because I have stopped trying to consciously think about the problem.

Have you ever struggled to think of an actor's name when you're watching a film only to have that name pop into your head ages later? When we stop trying to remember the name, our unconscious mind is free to keep searching.

The same thing happens when we write.

The more we try to think of something, the harder it becomes, so stop thinking for a while. Take the dog for a walk or tackle the ironing or the washing-up.

Another way to keep writer's block at bay is to do some writing exercises.

One that I find often works is to pick a character from your stock of photos and imagine that you are interviewing them. As you begin to ask them questions, you will start to build up a picture of the person, and ideas will start to form, without you even needing to try.

For examples of some of the questions you can ask, see the entry under Photographs.

Picking up where you left off can also be difficult.

One trick I've found very useful is to always stop before I want to, and just make a few notes about what I plan to write next. Then when I go back to that piece of writing I already know what's going to happen next.

Try it yourself sometime. You should find that once you get those first few sentences down, the rest will follow with far less effort.

Writing Magazines and Writers' Groups

I have subscribed to *Writers' Forum* and *Writers' News* for a number of years. Both magazines are packed with useful information.

They are also full of ideas.

Take *Writers' News/Writing Magazine*. Each month they have a short story competition with a set theme. To help readers come up with ideas, they offer hints as to what kind of story you might want to write.

For example, one month the competition theme was to write about a miser.

The magazine went on to explain that the word miser might be somebody who stockpiles ten pound notes under the mattress, or who is slow to buy their round at the pub. They said the person might be a typical mean old skinflint and pointed out that this term can be applied to people of any age.

This description makes an ideal prompt for a story idea, even if you don't want to enter the competition.

Writers' Forum also run regular competitions. The winning stories are published in the magazine. If the stories themselves don't inspire you, why not try reading the judge's comments instead? Like the blurb on a book, they will give you an idea of what the story is about so that you can write your own version.

I've had a column in *Writers' Forum* for some time now. It's called *Short Story Success*. In it, I tell readers something about my life as a full time writer, and offer advice and encouragement to them, so it's well worth buying the magazine just for that (and Paula Williams' *Ideas Square*, of course!)

Writing magazines are packed with useful articles ranging from those explaining how various authors found their inspiration, some even offer ready-made starting points for stories, plus there are all kinds of other useful titbits.

Another magazine that is well worth having a look at is *Mslexia*, which is aimed at female writers.

Mslexia offers a good mix of writing exercise and useful articles, plus regular competitions. You do have to be female to write for them though.

I can also recommend *The New Writer*.

If you take out a subscription, you will not only receive a well produced, informative magazine, you can also sign up for their email newsletter which is one of the best I've found. It's always crammed full of competition and other news and is very inspiring. They also run their own competitions, both serious and fun.

The National Association of Writers' Groups is also well worth joining. They produce a magazine for members as well as running competitions and organising an annual festival of writing.

What does this have to do with generating ideas? Nothing really, it's just that one of the best ways to hear about writing opportunities, competitions, and calls for anthology submissions is to meet other writers.

After all, there's no point in coming up with dozens of ideas if you can't think of anywhere to send the resulting stories.

If you don't belong to a group of any kind, my suggestion is join one as soon as possible. Take a look at the NAWG website and you will find a list of clubs and groups arranged geographically (www.nawg.co.uk).

There are so many benefits to belonging to a group of writers, not least making new friends. As a writer's life can be a lonely one, that has to be a good thing. I have belonged to various different groups and can honestly say that I learned something from each of them.

It's worth remembering that writers' groups vary enormously so if the first one you try doesn't suit you, don't let that put you off, try another one. There are dozens available online.

If all else fails, you can always start your own.

For help and advice, check the National Association of Writers' Groups' website.

Summary

By the time you reach the end of this book, your head should be buzzing with ideas. If it isn't, then you need to go through it again, more slowly.

Don't forget that learning how to come up with ideas is a skill. It takes time, patience and plenty of practise.

You will probably find that some methods work better for you than others, whilst some may not work at all. This is as it should be.

Fortunately, we are all unique. We come up with ideas in many different ways. All you have to do is find two or three methods that work for you and, like me, you will never run out of ideas for stories again.

Of course, once you have all these ideas, you need to be able to turn them into stories. That's what I will be looking at in my next book.

Meanwhile, keep writing, and remember, the more you do, the easier it becomes. Above all, writing fiction should be fun. If it isn't, you're doing something wrong.